Through The
FIRE

Marred Vessel, Yielded Vessel

by Vickie Faurie

Copyright © 2004 by Vickie Faurie
All Rights Reserved

All Scripture references are taken from the New International Version of the Bible, Copyright © 1973, 1978, 1984 by International Bible Society, Colorado Springs, Colorado unless otherwise noted.

McDougal Publishing is a ministry of The McDougal Foundation, Inc., a Maryland nonprofit corporation dedicated to spreading the Gospel of the Lord Jesus Christ to as many people as possible in the shortest time possible.

Published by:

McDougal Publishing
P.O. Box 3595
Hagerstown, MD 21742
www.mcdougalpublishing.com

ISBN 1-58158-077-0

Printed in the United States of America
For Worldwide Distribution

DEDICATED TO

My wonderful husband and beautiful children, for being a vital part of my life's journey.
To my Lord and Savior, for molding me upon the Potter's wheel, making me into a vessel for His use.

Acknowledgments

There are so many people who were greatly used by the hand of God and imparted God's Word into my life. In sincere gratitude to those who touched my life, I would like to acknowledge them for their part that God gave them in depositing into my life.

With gratitude to my husband, Gary, who truly is a rare gift from God given to me that I love and appreciate deeply. To my children, Adam and Melanie Faurie, Nathan and Elisabeth Hicks, treasured gifts from God, who continually remind me of God's goodness. To my beautiful grandchild, Taylor, who radiates with a childlike love. My gratitude to my parents, Delroy and Jean Kauke, for their faith in God.

I want to acknowledge the part that Kathryn Kuhlman had in my life and thank God for her being such a yielded loving vessel. I also want to acknowledge Richard and Lindsay Roberts and their encouragement, impartation and help to me. Pastors Billy Joe and Sharon Daugherty of Victory Christian Center, I will be forever grateful to the Lord for depositing you into my life, enriching me and allowing me to share God's Word. Thank you to Sid Roth and to Bob and Janie Duvall for their prayers, godly wisdom and friendship. To all who prayed, stood and believed the message God has unfolded needs to be published, so God can receive all the glory for the work of His hand in molding me. Special thank you to McDougal Publishing for their contribution in this project.

Most of all, I am eternally grateful to my Heavenly Father, who has molded me upon the potter's wheel and placed people in my life for an appointed time. And to the Lord Jesus Christ and the sweet Holy Spirit, who guide my steps daily as I run the race set before me.

Contents

1. The Witness 7
2. A New Day 19
3. Blessings and Sorrow 29
4. Marred Vessels 39
5. A Time to Reflect 49
6. The Journey Begins 57
7. Salted With Fire 65
8. Count It All Joy 73
9. Through It All 79
10. God Tested Us 85
11. The Mingled Life 91
12. The Greatest Gift 97
13. Surrendered Lives 101
14. A Changed Heart 105
15. Testimonies That Testify 109
16. Refined Like Silver 113
17. Reflections 117
18. Golden Grain 121
19. His Rose 125

Chapter One

THE WITNESS

I arrived at the scene of the burning convenience store just as the roof caved in. The stench of burning plastic permeated the air. In the background, I heard a series of small explosions, followed by another series of explosions. It sounded like someone was setting off a string of high-power fireworks. Later I learned that these were the stored soda cans exploding from the heat of the flaming rubble falling into their midst.

The building was in ruins. As I stood there, I wondered if there had been any survivors who had made it out of the store before the roof caved in. Suddenly, to my astonishment, I saw a woman walking out of the deadly flames and toxic smoke, carrying the still form of a small child.

Her face and small frame were darkened by soot, but the first thing that struck me was that she was not at all distressed. Shock, I thought at first glance, but then her gaze met mine and she smiled. I realized she wasn't in shock at all. She was at peace.

I looked back at the burned-out building. Hot spots of fire continued to rage in places. Even the heaps of fallen brick seemed to be ablaze.

How could she have walked through that fire of death to come out alive into the light of day? What obstacles did she have to overcome in order to survive, and how did she do it? It seemed impossible as one surveyed the ruins that she could still be standing, let alone walking out carrying a small child.

Through the dark soot, I saw that in her features there was a peace, as if an inner light shone through. There was no trace of the battle she must have fought to survive, no vain pride of the obvious courage it took to face the fear that must have paralyzed her as she faced the terror of her mortality, the panic over saving the child....

I marveled at the inner strength she must have had to face the agonizing pain and emerge from these fires of death, and I wanted to know where it came from. I coveted the strength to walk through a blazing fire and emerge into the light of day unscathed, and at peace.

The woman carried the child to the paramedics, who seemed to be startled into action by her arrival. No one had moved while she walked from the burning wreck of the building to the ambulance carrying the still form. Jolted into action, the paramedics quickly took the child and began examining it. I still didn't even know the gender of the child.

Coming out of shock myself, my reporter's mind began firing other questions: Why didn't anyone hear her screaming for help, or had she not even cried out for help? Where was her family? Hadn't anyone noticed she was missing? The questions were mounting in my mind and encircling me as I felt the need to have answers to this woman's story.

The paramedics were examining her carefully with looks of obvious astonishment on their faces. I knew that each baffled look told a story in itself of her miraculous condition.

I murmured out loud, "Miraculous."

The reporter in me screamed for me to rush over and begin the interview then and there. But something else had been stirred within me by that word *miraculous*, and whatever it was made me hesitate. She had emerged from the fires of death unscathed, and I wanted to know how she did it, not just for the story, but because I needed to know this secret of hers. I knew it was the secret we all search for when we face the flames of death in our own personal lives.

A throng of people had gathered and encircled the site, standing and wondering. The rescue squad, fire department, and police were all hard at work, working as a team. Though they operated smoothly, doing the work they were trained for, I could tell that each member of the team had been affected by this woman's survival. Occasionally I caught a glimpse of bewilderment on a firefighter's face, and more than once I saw a paramedic just standing there looking at her in amazement. The harsh reality of the burned-out building was undeniable, yet no one could doubt the fact that she had emerged without serious burns or injury.

How did she protect herself, or rather, who had protected her from this major disaster? Life had written her a major episode, which no one would have thought was possible to emerge from, yet she had, with tranquil peace, and even a smile for a stunned reporter watching on the side.

The rescue team was checking her again for any injuries and questioning her as I stood back taking everything in.

Suddenly the doors to the ambulance she was in were shut after one of the police officers entered the vehicle. They sat there for at least ten minutes before the policeman exited the vehicle. Then the rescue squad left abruptly, with sirens wailing and sped away into the distance as the woman and child were rushed to an emergency room somewhere in the city.

Questions were mounting again as I stood baffled by

this latest turn of events. I found myself thinking, "Only God knows exactly what's going on here." That was an odd thought, for me. I resigned myself to the fact that God had to have had a hand in this somehow.

Other stories I had witnessed and written about before started scrolling through my mind. Countless times I had stood as an "objective" witness to my fellow human beings receiving devastating news. I've seen the clench of fear that grips a mother when she's told that her only child, only twelve years old, has been killed by a reckless driver. I've seen the agony of loss when a father is informed that his son just killed a young lady.

Life's disappointments are all around as you hear the words of a doctor declare that your loved one is not expected to live. There are so many hidden little land mines sprawled out across life's field set to explode at any given moment. Waiting and watching is a wife who has been betrayed by her husband, crying in bitter disappointment. How does she keep going, when hit with such devastating news?

In times like these I've seen those who have defied all odds rise above the pain and agony, somehow passing through the valley of the shadow of death into victory. I've seen stories end in the triumph of the heart, and in the defeat of despair.

I sensed an urgency building within me. I needed to know more than just the details of this one event in this woman's life. Something had prepared her for this catastrophe. I needed to know more about the source of her hidden strength.

The story lay within the survivor, so I decided to follow after the ambulance in hopes of obtaining my story.

As I got into my car leaving the scene of what was a true miracle, I started questioning my motives. Why would this story affect me so differently than any other?

What had been so different about this story that would stir this desire in my heart to find an answer to this ultimate question? Normally, I would stay at the scene, question a few medics or police officers, and follow up in the morning at the hospital. I had reached a turning point, and although I couldn't put my finger on it at this moment, I knew that I was being driven by something more than the average touchy-feely local hero story this time.

I followed the ambulance to a local hospital where they suddenly opened the doors, and out she came. She was quickly walked to the emergency room, then wheeled off into a room where emergency workers started questioning her.

I decided I would stay put and retrieve my story as soon as I was allowed to talk with her. It seemed to be such a long wait, but emergency room procedures never seem quick. While I sat there waiting, the desire to know what was going on built up within me.

Soon family members began arriving to find out how she was doing. Within the next hour, I had the opportunity to speak briefly with her husband. He informed me that I could speak with her the next morning at their home. She was fine.

He told me that she was being released from the hospital and would be available for questioning the next morning. I didn't hesitate to set up an appointment for ten o'clock the next morning. As quickly as he appeared, he was gone, heading back towards the emergency room and her.

I asked a nurse about the child, and after she learned I was a reporter and checked my credentials, I found out that the child wasn't the woman's, just a local kid who had been buying some candy with his allowance. He had passed out from smoke inhalation, but was in stable condition and was expected to fully recover. No one doubted that this mysterious woman had saved his young life.

With this momentary postponement, I reassessed my options. If I hurried, I could make it back to the scene of the fire, and possibly get some details of the story from any eyewitnesses.

As I approached the scene of the fire, I saw that almost everyone had left, and that the officials had put up yellow warning ribbon around the area.

I knew my camera crew had captured the event on video and taken pictures, but I wanted to know more.

I stepped out from my car and surveyed the ruins. It hit me again that it was truly a miracle that anyone could have survived this inferno. Steam was still rising from the site. Piles of twisted metal and melted glass littered the landscape. Two walls had collapsed. There were a few loiterers, but no one was passing the yellow tape. I recognized the type: virtual vultures, drawn to the scene of a horrifying disaster, taking mental snapshots that they could trot out over tomorrow's coffee at the office. The witnesses were gone.

Gone too were the local news teams. One media van remained, and I was pleasantly surprised to see it belonged to my photographic partner, Tom. I called his name and waved to get his attention.

He glanced up, and seeing me, he motioned for me to come over. I hoped that he had had the opportunity to capture some of the on-site story while I was chasing my strange compulsion.

We talked and decided we would discuss the whole matter over a cup of coffee. As I followed him to a little café down the street, I was eager to hear what he had discovered. The café was a perfect place—it offered private booths, and we arrived between the afternoon and evening rushes.

As we sat down to enjoy our cup of coffee and trade stories, we both sensed this was no ordinary story. We both had been witnesses to a miracle and knew that we wanted answers to this story.

Immediately Tom asked me, "Where did you go?"

I told him that I'd felt compelled to follow the woman to see if I could interview her. I also wanted to get the official report on any injuries, any treatment, and whether she would be released as quickly as it seemed that she would.

Tom asked, "So, was she injured or not?"

I responded, "She is just fine and is being released today."

Tom settled back, and seemed content with that piece of information. He absently sipped his coffee, and I could see that he was mentally going over the shots he had just taken, putting together his photojournalistic presentation. Later, we would put together a brief item that might hit the papers, or make it to the local news if there wasn't a national emergency to address. No fatalities, no big news.

"I'm interviewing her tomorrow," I said.

Tom looked up, interrupted in his mental editing, surprised at my statement.

"Why would you want to do that, Annee? This isn't a major story. She made it through a fire. A quick visual with a nice voice-over on the ten-o'clock news is all it merits, two or three paragraphs of filler in the local section of the papers. People see this stuff all the time. Where's the story?

I could tell that he hadn't been affected the way I had by this tragedy. He saw the events, but not the story underneath.

"Tom," I said, "it's a miracle! She wasn't harmed at all. You saw the wreck that she just walked out of, calm, cool, and collected, as if the roof hadn't just collapsed around her."

"Sure, a miracle," he said, "but it happens every day, in every city around the world. Readers and listeners don't care about the details; they just want to see a fire, a survivor, and a rescued kid to make them think the world's an alright place to be sometimes. Keep it nice, keep it neat."

"I know, Tom, I know," I said. He was right, but there it was, that churning in my gut that wouldn't let me just walk away, with only the surface facts of this story.

"Tom, I just have to go on this; you know a good reporter can't ignore her gut feeling. There's more to this than you see."

Whatever Tom's reply might have been was lost when his cell phone started ringing. It was the office telling him to come in immediately. Within a few seconds, my cell phone rang also. The other teams had returned from this story while I was still at the hospital, and my editor wanted to know what was keeping me.

I told her I had just sat down to discuss the story with Tom and that we were at a local café. Tom had already paid the bill and was heading out the door of the café. I said I had a different angle on this, and that there was more to it than met the eye at first glance. I could tell she was puzzled, so I told her I would explain it when I got into the office.

As I left the café, I wondered whether I'd get the opportunity to hear Tom's side of this story before it was released.

On the way back to the office, it occurred to me that this was the first time my editor had questioned my judgment on a story. I had always brought a complete story that was well reported and finely edited over the years, but I couldn't deny that this story had an unusual grip on me. I wondered myself where this was coming from.

I finally reached the office and decided I'd stand my ground; I had to know more and follow this story through from beginning to end.

As I stepped into the newsroom, the receptionist told me that my editor expected me to report directly to her. For the first time in years, I felt butterflies in my stomach as I walked through the corridors to her office.

I wasn't reassured when I saw her face. Her usual openness to my story lines was gone. She looked downright stern. She had me close the door behind me.

"Annee, would you care to explain to me why you chased after an ambulance instead of interviewing witnesses at the scene on this story? It's really not like you."

The next half hour was the most grueling I had faced since taking this position. I tried to explain the strange compulsion that had gripped me. I told her about the look of serenity that was on the woman's face, the smile she flashed me as she walked out of the burning rubble, the sense of the miraculous that suffused the scene, heightened by the fact that despite the horrors she faced, she escaped unscathed.

Instead of the understanding I had hoped for, her face went from stern to concerned. She tried to talk me out of it, to get me to see that this was just another fire story, but I firmly stood my ground. I knew there was more to this story than the obvious facts. I had to have the answers to the burning questions that her survival had ignited in me.

"Annee, you know I've always been completely honest about what I think about your work. Frankly, I'm worried about you. You've been working too hard, and you're starting to get a little frayed at the edges."

I didn't respond. I had made my case, and I was determined to pursue this story, no matter what the consequences might be.

She must have seen the determination on my face. She sighed, and said, "Alright, Annee, you've got two weeks' leave. Take this time to go after this mysterious story of yours, but while you're off, get some rest. You need it."

Leaving her office, my confidence was restored. She might not have seen the story within the story, but I knew that there was something in this that would have a real impact, something that could change people's lives for the better.

I hoped to catch up with Tom to compare notes, but when I went to his cubicle, he was engrossed in his work. He had a story to get out, a deadline to meet, and he was going with what he knew. He didn't have an invisible drive to get beneath the surface of this story, and I knew it was pointless to disturb him.

It was strange. I had never had a hunch that didn't turn out to be pure gold. Somehow I just wasn't being heard on this quite yet, but I knew that in due time this hunch of mine could make a real difference. It had meaning, I thought.

I felt a mixture of disappointment and relief. Tom and I had developed a good working relationship, and we produced high-quality stories together. I wanted him to have the opportunity to find out what was behind this miracle that had unfolded before our eyes. So there was disappointment, but at the same time, I was relieved that my editor hadn't squashed the story outright.

Despite the disappointment, excitement was building inside me as I turned my attention to tomorrow's interview. Looking at my watch, I was surprised to find that it was already past five. So much had taken place that I hadn't noticed how late it had become.

I had so much left to do to get ready for the interview. I grabbed a bite to eat on the way home, and started preparing my questions over a wax paper-wrapped cheeseburger and greasy french fries.

I knew I had to prove to my editor that my hunch wasn't baseless. That sharpened my focus, but I knew that what was driving me was more than making a point to my boss. Something in me needed the answers to these questions.

Chapter Two

A New Day

I was awakened the next morning by the sunlight streaming through my bedroom window. It poured in and seemed to dance about the room, celebrating a new day. Catching the mood, I found myself fully awake, and as if in response, my thoughts leaped ahead in anticipation of the day's events.

I quickly jumped out of bed and got ready for the interview. I put my carefully prepared questions in my briefcase, checked the tape and batteries of my recorder, and made sure I had a notepad and two working pens. Something inside told me that this was the most important interview I would ever have, and I didn't want any unlooked-for obstacles getting in my way.

I took a deep breath as I went over my mental checklist one last time. I had everything I needed, and I was ready to go. Soon I would be meeting the woman who seemed to have the key to unlocking the answers to so many questions.

As I drove to her home, I realized that this interview wasn't likely to be the last. There was something inside of me holding itself in check. Whatever lay behind that hold was full of hope, expectation, and raw curiosity.

It didn't take long to get to her home; rather, it didn't

seem to take very long. As I drove, new questions kept popping into my mind, and I soon lost track of time.

When I arrived at her home, she greeted me with a warm, kind smile and invited me to come in.

My introduction seemed clumsy, not at all what I had hoped for, and I quickly found myself being swept into the kitchen of her home.

She had set the kitchen table with a steaming teakettle, two cups and pastries. I wasn't used to such sudden hospitality from the subjects of my interviews. Usually it takes time to break the ice, to establish common ground before delving into the very personal details of the circumstances of life that make up a story. I was taken aback, and most of my expectations had already evaporated. I hadn't even gotten her name yet.

I was trying to regain my composure when she said, "I've been expecting you."

"Oh, yes," I found myself saying, "your husband told you I would be here this morning."

She smiled a warm and relaxed smile.

"Yes, but I knew the moment I saw you, when I was coming out of that little store, that you and I would be speaking soon. God has a way of putting things within us, so that we just know."

Slowly I nodded my head in acknowledgment, realizing suddenly that I wasn't the one in control here. With an internal sigh, I mentally trashed my rehearsal of the morning's events and resigned myself to the fact that I would spend most of my time listening rather than asking questions.

It was a strange experience. I was used to being the one in control of an interview, but like so many other details in this story, this was going to be something new to me. It wasn't easy relinquishing control, but I soon found myself settling back into the chair and enjoying the tea and pastries as she began to talk.

She seemed at such peace as she started to explain to me that it would be best to start from the beginning. She said, "Life can be full of pain, frustration, misery, and constant struggles when we don't know who God made us to be."

It was an odd way to start an interview, I found myself thinking, but at the same time I knew that this was how it was supposed to be. I sipped my tea as she continued.

"Many times in life we try to be someone else, not asking God for guidance through life's trials and difficulties. Becoming the person God created often will take you on the road of affliction before you submit to the blessed Savior in obedience."

She paused a moment, as if listening, and then went on.

"God doesn't allow us to suffer without a reason. Usually, the reason is hidden from us at first, but before we even realize we're in trouble, He's already working out His purpose and plan for whatever we're facing. We need to trust Him completely when we can't see our way through the darkness surrounding us, knowing He's always with us and that He does only what's best for us."

My face must have betrayed my puzzlement. She took a deep breath and sighed compassionately.

"Maybe I'm getting ahead of myself here." She smiled that same inviting smile that seemed to shine up out of her soul at me that I had seen the day before.

"I'm sorry. Let me properly introduce myself. I'm Vickie Faurie, the woman you saw walk out of a fiery furnace to see the light of day without a burn or scratch on her. I know that's why you're here, but that's not the story you're really looking for. The story I have to tell isn't about me at all. This story is about the awesomeness of God. So forgive me if at times I don't do what is customary or proper, so to speak. What I have to share is a story of trials, tribulation, despair, loss, and agony, yet at the same time it's a story of joy and victory, truth and confidence, and above all, a story of the peace that surpasses all understanding."

She looked at me intently, and I felt uncomfortable for a moment. I wondered if my discomfort was how the subjects of my own interviews felt when I started hitting them with my meticulously refined questions.

"You did come here for the complete story, didn't you?" she asked.

Quickly I responded, seeing my window of opportunity opening. "Oh, yes; nothing else will do."

Somehow I found myself telling her about the odd compulsion I had been under since seeing her walk out of that building alive and smiling at me, about my editor's concern, and about my two-week vacation to pursue the underlying story.

"Fine," she replied. "Let's start today with the beginning of my life's journey."

She went on to tell me that she had been born in Waukegan, Illinois, to her parents, Delroy and Jean Kauke, the third child out of four. Her family wasn't wealthy by any means. In fact, they were below average income. Her earliest memory was of living in a shabby little house, with mice running about. The house should probably have been condemned. Fortunately, her grandfather was building a better house for them on the lot next door to the shack they called home.

She remembered life had been hard at times. She remembered that she was usually hungry and that the winters were cold. But as she grew older, things seemed to improve somewhat.

At the age of eight, she had accepted the Lord into her heart. She was attending a Baptist church when she heard that Jesus Christ, the only begotten Son of God, had gone to the cross to pay the price for her personal sins. The Spirit stirred her then, and she found herself going forward in response to that call. She knew that she needed God, even at that young age.

"God knows all things," she told me, "and He is with us through all things, no matter how dark. His Word says He will never leave us or forsake us. He called to me then, depositing His Holy Spirit in me, and although I didn't fully grasp the power, I know that the only reason I got through what followed was His grace."

She went on to tell me that as a young child, the teenage children of a family her parents were trying to help had sexually assaulted her. To keep her quiet about the episode, they'd hung her out an open window of the second story of their house and threatened to drop her onto the concrete drive if she ever said anything. This was only one of their many methods of torture to keep her from revealing the episode. She kept the secret, even though she and her parents visited with them regularly. She never told her parents what took place; she was ashamed and frightened back then. As she grew older, she saw how the devil was deceiving her, and how he planned to destroy her by keeping her shackled to the fear and guilt.

"But time was, and still is, in God's hands. He eventually healed me of those pains from my childhood. I'm not the only one to fall into the fires of sexual abuse, rape, and verbal abuse," she said. "People need to be ministered to, by men and women of God. I finally shared that incident with my parents later in life, and just by bringing this dark secret to the light, Satan's hold over me was broken. My wound was healed, and I was freed from his bondage.

"Pretending that nothing occurred will not heal the situation," she went on. "All that does is fuel the fires of distrust inside. I've found that we need to seek the Lord. He guides us, directs our steps so that we find godly people who can walk us through the healing waters.

"We can't anticipate or protect ourselves from every disaster lurking around the corner; but at the same time, we can't begin to imagine the blessings waiting for us, even if the journey to the blessings takes us through the very shadows of death. So many are crying out, 'Help me, O Lord my God, for I am needy; my heart is wounded deep within; I am an object of scorn.' And God is replying today, 'I will be with you in trouble; I will deliver you; put your trust in Me.'"

Vickie paused, and we both sat there in silence. She was still at peace, and I could see that her words about being healed must have been sincere. There was no hurt left in the memories; she was fully focused on how God had brought her through these fires.

My thoughts started to drift toward the fires I had passed through, toward that darkness in the center of my being, and I felt my innermost self crying out desperately for what she had.

I shook my head; this wasn't the time or the place to revisit the graveyard of my past.

Vickie saw me shake my head, and it seemed to bring her back to the present, to the interview that was going on. She smiled, and continued telling me her story.

Life had dealt her things that she never could have imagined, though through the events she faced she learned to trust God and to esteem Him greatly.

At twelve years old she was still attending the Baptist church with her parents. Now a new page was turned. Vickie became critically ill.

It started out as an intense itching in her feet. She frequently ran around barefoot, and it was possible that she had just stumbled through something outside. When she got home, she washed her feet well. The itching didn't stop.

By bedtime she had washed her feet a couple of times, and now her mother had her scrubbing them again. The next day she was taken to the doctor, who gave her some anti-itch cream. That didn't work either.

As time went on, her parents took her to see doctor after doctor, to no avail. The disabling sickness kept getting progressively worse.

Soon the itching became so severe that it affected her nervous system. Pains shot through her limbs like electric currents, and she wasn't able to eat or keep food down.

Her frail body began shutting down. Her limbs curled up, and she couldn't walk or write. Soon she could only be moved by wheelchair. At night, she couldn't sleep more than a couple of hours due to the pain racking her small body.

Out of desire to be relieved from her pain, she began earnestly praying that the Lord would let her die so she could go to Heaven.

It was evident that she was dying. The doctors had given up any hope for her survival, telling her parents that there was nothing more they could do for her. When she was sent home the last time from the hospital, her parents were told that it was time to prepare for her burial.

Vickie fell silent again, and the expression on her face told me that she was reliving those memories of pain. As she had spoken in her strong, warm voice, I had experienced with her these tragedies, and my own heart was responding to the pain that she must have felt. But again, I saw that inner peace shining through her features.

She must have read the compassion on my face.

"Don't you worry, hon. God had a plan for me. You didn't see a cripple wheeled out of that burning wreck, did you?"

She laughed, and I found myself laughing too.

"There I was at home, waiting, and even hoping to die, when God intervened. Word had come that Kathryn Kuhlman was coming to Chicago. When my parents heard this, they began making plans to get me to her service. News of Kathryn Kuhlman's healing services was spreading like wildfire through the church, especially among the network of those afflicted with sickness and disease. The Holy Spirit had brought healing to His people, and He used Kathryn Kuhlman as His vessel."

She took a moment to refresh our tea, and gathered her thoughts before going on.

"You know, I remember that day so clearly. It was October 13, 1971, at McCormick's Place, in Chicago. When we arrived, the main auditorium was already filled, so we were seated in an overflow room. I had absolutely refused to bring my wheelchair, so my parents carried me in and got me seated in the most comfortable position possible.

"Sitting there in the overflow room, I looked around at all the other people who had come to the service to be healed. My own pain seemed small to me then, and I began praying for those around me to be healed."

Vickie paused briefly, and I saw a fierce joy shining through her eyes when she continued.

"All of a sudden a bolt of heat went through my entire body. It started at the top of my head and went out through my feet. Instantly my curled up, crippled limbs went perfectly straight, and I jumped to my feet.

"One of Kathryn Kuhlman's attendants saw what had happened, and the next thing I knew, she was talking to us, praising God, and leading us to the main auditorium."

She smiled in glee as the memory took her back to that time.

"God healed me instantly, in the twinkling of an eye. One minute I was sitting there, a crippled girl brought to a healing service with the look of death in my limbs and features, and the next I was walking, healed completely, and made whole!

"See," she said, suddenly looking intensely into my eyes, "what Satan had meant for evil, God took and turned around for good, receiving all the glory and praise in the process. Do you see?"

While she had been talking, I had felt the air grow heavier in the room, and though there were no fresh-cut flowers in that kitchen, I found memories of the sweet smells of spring passing through my mind. I didn't see what she was talking about, but I knew that there was something to be seen, if only I had the eyes to see it.

Vickie went on before I could answer, or even question her about what she had experienced.

"They led us to the stage, and my parents were given a chance to share about what had just taken place. Kathryn Kuhlman came over to talk with me about it, and as soon as she came close, I fell to the floor under the power of God. It was thick, heavy, and absolutely wonderful. When I had managed to get up again, Kathryn tried to ask me some questions, but again, as soon as she approached, I went down. This happened each time she tried to talk to me about the healing. I don't know why, but I do know it served God's plan for us that night.

"God had truly touched me, for my limbs were perfectly straight, and I could *run* again. Jesus came that day 'that I might have life, and life more abundantly.' That's John 10:10, paraphrased. I discovered many things through this experience. Not only was I physically transformed, but both of my fully functioning feet had been placed on a road that would lead to spiritual transformation and healing as well."

Vickie fell silent, and we both sat there.

I began to think about how young she was then, and yet she had already faced two major tragedies in her brief life. I was amazed at the strength she must have had, even then. I was even more amazed at how God had put His hand into her life.

Her talk about God's plan and His blatant intervention in her life made me start wondering about this interview, and where exactly I was headed, and who might be orchestrating this interview behind the scenes.

I glanced at my watch and saw that our allotted time had run out long ago. We sat sipping our tea, and made arrangements for our next meeting. I was looking forward to it. The anticipation I had felt before was nothing compared to what I felt now. I wanted to know what else God had done in her life to turn a wounded cripple into the graceful woman sitting before me. I also wanted to know what He might have in store for me.

Chapter Three

BLESSINGS AND SORROW

The next day dawned bright and glorious, and again I quickly got dressed and ready.

As I sat reviewing my notes from the day before, great excitement was building within me. I didn't prepare any questions this time. I had come to the realization as I slept that I was there by divine appointment from God. As I began to leave, I reached for my umbrella, for the skies had become overcast and it looked like it was going to rain.

As I pulled into her driveway, it seemed different for me than it had the day before. I was more settled, quietly anticipating what today held in store.

Entering her home, I heard the sound of music quietly playing in the background. It seemed to be a song of redemption. She graciously invited me to come sit with her in the living room. There was such a sense of peace in her home, and I felt comfortably at ease.

After we sat down and I prepared to take my notes, she began.

"Today I want to share about how blessings can turn to sorrow, when not understood."

This was a surprising comment, but I was certain she would explain.

We quickly recapped her being healed by God so we could pick up where we left off.

"Yes," she said, "that was an amazing miracle God

gave me, and I was very excited. The story of my undeniable healing spread quickly through my church. At first, I was going around to various churches telling everybody about the wonderful miracle that I had received, and I thought it would bring joy and kindle a passion for our loving God in those who heard it.

"To my surprise, however, I began receiving harsh replies. Some people refused to believe it, and tried to come up with some other explanation for what had happened. They grew vehement in their attacks, and my joy quickly turned to sorrow. Instead of standing up for what God had done, I stopped sharing the gift I had received. I was so young, and didn't understand that some would close their eyes and ears to what God had done for me. Though I cherished the day He healed me, I kept it as a gift within myself.

"But God was stirring up a hunger in me for more of Him. I wasn't being fulfilled in my spiritual walk by staying at that church. At school, I had a friend who attended an Assembly of God church, who was not only accepting of the miracle but also overjoyed by God's gift to me. When I confided to her the persecution I had gone through, she invited me to come to one of their services."

Vickie smiled, pausing in her narrative.

"Let me tell you, Anne, this church service was so different from what I was used to seeing at my church. People were talking in strange languages, worshiping God with their hands lifted up in the air, and really getting into enjoying the presence of our awesome God. Quietly, I watched closely as they seemed to give praise to God. They weren't just talking about what God was doing in their hearts and lives; they were praising Him for it.

"I felt the Holy Spirit then, like a warm breath coming down from God, raising the hairs on my arms and filling me with a joy I had never felt before. I felt something inside of me, something that had been longing for release, come to the surface. Words like those the other people were speaking began forming in the back of my mind, and I opened my mouth and gave voice to them. A long stream of words that I didn't recognize came pouring out of my mouth, and it didn't bother me, I wasn't ashamed or embarrassed. I was caught up in the Spirit, giving God praise in a language that only He could understand."

I sat there watching Vickie speak. I had heard of the gift of tongues, but I had written it off as emotionalism, a nice thing for the people who believed in it, but not really something that was of God. I knew that the people in Acts had received the gift of tongues, but I didn't think it was really necessary for today. But as I watched her, I saw that Vickie had obviously experienced something profound, and combined with her inner peace and my own experience the day before, I wasn't able to just write it off as a nice delusion.

Vickie continued.

"In the excitement of this newfound experience, I went home to share it with my parents. I also decided to inform my Baptist friends at church about this wonderful experience, and I'm sure you can imagine it didn't go over so well. That church didn't believe that the gift of tongues was for today. They believed that all the supernatural gifts of the Spirit were given to the apostles and were only intended to form the church. How they reconciled my obvious healing with this doctrine, I don't know.

"But Dad was the head deacon and well respected within the church. It wasn't long before he was questioned about what I was talking about. Rather than cause an upheaval in the Baptist church over this event, I decided to leave the church. My parents came to visit the church I was attending, and it transformed them as well. That was a very happy time in my life.

Vickie paused and took a sip of water, collecting her thoughts.

"What happened next confused me for a long time. God was moving in that Assembly of God church, and He was present and active in the lives of most of the families that attended. But the youth of the church weren't in tune with God, despite witnessing His hand at work in their lives. They were caught up in the things of the world. These were people my own age, people I quickly became friends with.

"Less than a year after being healed and receiving the gift of tongues, I drifted away from that close encounter with my Holy God. My relationships with my friends, and the lifestyles we were leading, became more important to me than my relationship with God. I did have the Spirit of God in me, but I still fell into the trap of alcohol, smoking, and experimenting with drugs. I soon became depressed, in spite of the 'fun' I was having. I wasn't serving God at all.

"This went on for about six months, when suddenly I felt compelled to cry out to God to deliver me. I needed a change in my life, and only God could bring it about. Adolescent pressures had mounted, and I desperately needed to have someone in my life. Overwhelmed with adolescence, I felt plain, small, and not pretty.

"On December 31 at a youth lock-in, I met the man I was going to marry. He was tall, dark-haired, green-eyed, and ever so kind. Watching him play basketball against the other churches was exciting; he was so athletic. That evening our church won the trophy, mostly because he was so good at what he did. I met him, and we talked, and eventually exchanged nametags and phone numbers. After the lock-in, I spent days waiting to hear from him. Finally, he called."

Vickie took another sip of water, enjoying the memory of falling in love.

"We went out a few times, and it was apparent that God was starting the next stage of work in my life. This young man was a new Christian with strong standards about not smoking, drinking, or doing drugs. It was like music to my ears. I needed a person of strong character in my life. I was escaping into the distractions of the world to deal with my past pain instead of seeking God. Then He brought someone into my life who would change my focus, and direct me back to the only source of healing."

Vickie paused again. "Let's get something straight," she said. "I don't mean that when someone's hurting and wounded and scarred from the flames of life that they should go around looking for someone to come along and make everything better. There is no man out there who can fulfill all your needs; only God can fulfill an individual. God used this man to bring me to a different stage in my walk with Him, but it was God who did the changing, not the man. God's love is mighty, awesome, and truly life-transforming as we grow in the light of Him."

Vickie then continued with her story.

"Within a couple of weeks of dating we became engaged. Life was looking good; he was charming, kind, and understanding. I was young, and deeply in love. As we grew closer, we found ourselves facing the temptations every couple must face. The flames of our passion burned hot, and it wasn't long before we fell into the snare of the enemy and had premarital sex."

Vickie looked at me thoughtfully. "You know, people

today don't really understand what sin does. God made us to be vessels, just like a bowl or a pitcher, to be filled with His Spirit and used for His purposes. Our sins mar the vessels. Even though He loves us and forgives us when we fall into sin, every sin we fall into leaves its mark, a scar that the enemy will use in his attacks against us.

"The scars of sin marred our vessels as we surrendered to sexual impurity. The Holy Spirit brought us to conviction, and we repented, but only time could wash away the stains of shame we had brought into our lives."

I had a question at this point. "Vickie, when we fall into sin, and become marred, does that mean we'll be marred forever? Does it hinder God's plan for us?"

Vickie laughed. "Anne, that's a good question. You must be careful not to fall into the web of lies the enemy spins. God will grant you the courage to confess your sins truthfully, if you ask Him to, and that truthfulness destroys the web of deceit the enemy spins. God can and will transform your past sins and pain from marred scars to beautiful rays of light. Godly men and women in the Bible such as David and Bathsheba, Rahab the harlot, and Mary Magdalene were all marred vessels. Their scars became badges of victory as they walked through the fires of life, displaying their lives to all as an example of how God takes tragedy and turns it into triumph. Satan tries to hit you with a deathblow of shame, disgrace, and despair, to paralyze you. But when you acknowledge your past sins, and give God the glory for triumphing over the devil, you'll find that God transforms your past scars into stars. Look here."

She opened a worn Bible to Psalm 9:9-10, and read: "The LORD is a refuge for the oppressed, a stronghold in times of trouble. Those who know your name will trust in you, for you, LORD, have never forsaken those who seek you."

She looked at me, and I grew uncomfortable, sure that she was seeing into the darkness inside of me. Sensing the discomfort, she smiled, and said, "Anne, you can believe what it says. He is our refuge, a mighty stronghold in times of trouble."

Somehow that made sense to me on a deep level, and I relaxed. This woman had been through fires, I could tell. I sensed that she wouldn't condemn me if she knew about my own past, that she would understand.

Vickie went on with her story.

"We married in about six months after we met, at our local church. We blissfully settled into our small apartment and began the years-long process of adjusting to each other's little annoying habits. It became quite testing at times, as in any relationship, but we worked through it all.

"Not long after we were married, we received a call with news that Gary's dad had died from Lou Gehrig's disease. Gary had not seen his dad since he was twelve years old; his dad had left the family due to his illness. It was important for Gary to attend the funeral; he had to release the pain that was within his heart. Gary was the oldest boy out of seven children, which seemed to make it even harder for him. It took a long time for Gary to wrestle out his pain with God, but eventually God healed the pain from the loss of not having a father figure in his life.

"Time passed, and soon we were expecting our first child. Anticipation grew as the day of his birth drew closer. Then, he came into the world in the midst of one of the worst snowstorms in history, with snowdrifts as high as eight feet. Even getting to the hospital was a challenge. Thankfully we made it to the hospital before the full storm was unleashed. Beautiful blue eyes, blond hair, and perfect in our eyes was Adam Daniel, our firstborn child. That was truly a day of blessing for us. Little did we know how close we were to being hit with yet more sorrow.

"We were getting ready to head home when I learned that my brother had been charged as an accessory to armed robbery and was in prison. The crime was committed the day our son was born. It just goes to show how the enemy is always trying to thwart God's plan. Within a short time, my brother was sentenced to prison for his crime. Life had taken on a new meaning; the Lord will bless even in the midst of sorrow."

It had begun to rain outside, and the sound of the falling rain reminded me of the song "Showers of Blessing." The skies were dark, casting a shadow of despair, and yet the rain was refreshing the earth once again. It seemed to fit so perfectly with what she had shared today. In the darkness, joy can be found.

Our time came to an end. I gathered up my notes and tape recorder and got ready to leave, thanking her again for her time and telling her how much I looked forward to our next meeting.

As I was heading towards the door, Vickie reached out and held my hand, drawing my gaze into her eyes.

Anne," she said, "I assure you, prayer and time heals marred vessels." Giving my hand a squeeze, she said, "Remember that."

I wondered what it was she saw when she looked at me. Had God told her something, whispered words into her heart just for me? Something was stirring in my heart.

I just nodded my head in agreement and then quickly left. I wasn't ready to reveal myself to her.

Driving home, I cried out to God, begging Him not

to expose any hidden areas of my life. I needed that part to stay hidden. I didn't want those old wounds exposed, those scars and mars revealed to the world. I couldn't stand the persecution I might endure, from others or from myself.

Vickie knew I was struggling with my past issues, but I refused to open myself up. I had seen firsthand the tremendous persecution others had to endure as they laid themselves open for brutal attacks. Shaking off my fears and the strange feelings I was having, I resolved not to look to her for help over my past. I was just here for the story, I reminded myself, and shrugged off any further thought about my own scars.

Chapter Four

MARRED VESSELS

The next day I returned to Vickie Faurie's home, mentally prepared to keep my emotions out of the interview. My resolve the previous afternoon to ignore my pain hadn't been sufficient for keeping me from struggling with haunting memories. All her talk about God at work had begun to raise a different emotion in my heart, and before I had fallen asleep, I had cried out again to God, this time in anger, yelling at Him for what He had allowed to happen in my life. I was shocked at the depth of my rage, and I went on railing against God for a long time. I had finally fallen asleep, sobbing into my pillow.

When the morning came, I had managed to pull myself together, to put on my "reporter face" again. I was sure I was ready to just get the story.

After we were ready to continue with the interview, Vickie astonished me with words that cut right to my heart.

"Who are we to question God, and how He makes us? Do we give orders to God about the works of His hands? Who are we, to talk back to God?"

She looked at me, seeing my mask fall. She offered me a glass of water, which I gratefully accepted, taking the time to get my composure back. Peeved, I asked myself exactly who was being interviewed here.

Then she opened her Bible and read to me the following passages: Isaiah 45:9 and 11, Romans 9:19-20, and Isaiah 29:15-16.

"Woe to him who quarrels with his Maker, to him who is but a potsherd among potsherds on the ground. Does the clay say to the potter, 'What are you making?' Does your work say, 'He has no hands'? ...or give me orders about the work of my hands?"

"'For who resists his will?' But who are you, O man, to talk back to God? 'Shall what is formed say to him who formed it, why did you make me like this?'"

"Woe to those who go to great depths to hide their plans from the LORD, who do their work in darkness and think, 'Who sees us? Who will know?' You turn things upside down, as if the potter were thought to be like the clay! Shall what is formed say to him who formed it, 'He did not make me'? Can the pot say of the potter, 'He knows nothing'?"

When she finished, she looked up at me, saying, "I have often questioned God and resisted Him; therefore it has resulted in me becoming a marred vessel."

I was suddenly relieved. It wasn't about me at all; she was just going on with her story.

"The Bible is full of marred vessels," she said. "There was Saul who became Paul, Mary Magdalene who had seven demons cast out of her, and Peter who denied Christ. Even Job questioned God's right to test him."

She turned to her Bible, and starting in Job 35:16, read to me about how Elihu spoke the truth to Job, who opened his mouth with empty words. Without knowledge he multiplied words. She went on to read God's reply in Job 38:2-3: "Who is this that darkens my counsel with words without knowledge? Brace yourself like a man: I will question you, and you shall answer me."

Then she turned to Job's reply to God in chapter 42:2-6: "I know that you can do all things; no plan of yours can be thwarted. You asked, 'Who is this that obscures my counsel without knowledge?' Surely I spoke of things I did not understand, things too wonderful for me to know. You said, 'Listen now, and I will speak: I will question you, and you shall answer me.' My ears have heard of you but now my eyes have seen you. Therefore I despise myself and repent in dust and ashes."

Vickie looked up at me. "How often do we question God about Him testing us, God examining or evaluating what is really in our hearts? We aren't even able to hold a candle to Job. He was upright, blameless; he feared God and shunned evil. Yet when he faced the trials, we find that Job spoke without knowledge, his words lacked insight. He might be tested to the utmost for answering like a wicked man; to his sin he added rebellion, multiplying his words against God. See, before being tested, Job seemed to be one way, but when tested, we find that he was one who spoke without knowledge and in his heart was rebellious towards God. Job 3:25 shows the heart of Job revealed.

What I feared has come upon me; what I dreaded has happened to me.

However, once Elihu drew this to his attention and God confronted Job, he repented in dust and ashes.

"Just as Job, we still question God today, opening our mouths and speaking without knowledge.

"God knows how many times I've done it, Anne," Vickie said. "I found myself walking through the trials of life, when the fire seemed to be blazing all around and the pain so intense, without even a fraction of God's knowledge, and I screamed out against Him, yelling, 'Why, God?'

"Gary and I had been married for four years. I thought life was going fine. We had our beautiful child, and although there were some minor issues in our marriage, I was confident that they were things that every married couple went through. I would have said that overall our life was full of joy. Then in one day, all my joy turned to sorrow and betrayal. I learned that my husband was being unfaithful in our marriage.

"I was devastated. Confronting him, he told me it was the truth. The words rang in my ears; it seemed to be a nightmare.

"Anne, nothing had ever hurt like that. This was worse than being molested, worse than being crippled. I had trusted my husband. The pain was so great that I ran down the street in hopes of being killed by some passing automobile. However, God had His hand upon me as I was pulled back away from the street to safety.

"The agony of betrayal had laid me wide open. I quickly prayed to God to deliver me from this pain. At that moment, I couldn't see how God could have had His hand on me in that situation. Nevertheless, God told me to forgive and love unconditionally. The struggle was great within me, and I tell you, there were days when I felt like getting even. Thankfully, there were other days, days when I could just rest in the words God gave me. A great battle was being fought within and around me during that time. Rebuilding our shattered relationship wasn't easy. But God had a plan, and through this trial in life I would grow."

I watched Vickie closely, looking for any hint of remaining pain over her betrayal. She sat there, aware of my scrutiny, and gently smiled. The pain that it must have caused her was truly gone. She went on with her story.

"Time passed, and God blessed us with a second

child who enriched our lives. She was a beautiful, brown-eyed baby girl, with a cream-colored complexion. The Lord impressed me to name her Elisabeth De Anne . She was a joyful little girl. Life had changed once again, and there was renewed hope as I watched our children grow and play. They became like medicine from God as I listened to them laugh, play ,or sing, never being concerned about anything.

"Adam was strong-willed, certain, and bold. Elisabeth was joyful and compassionate. Both of them were strong in character, and as I taught them the lessons of life, God used them to teach me as well. I spent so many hours in prayer that they would continue to hear my words echo through their lives long after they left our home. I knew then, as now, that only time would tell as they too walked through tests, trials, and persecution in this life. I kept praying that they would see God's hand directing them as He has directed me. Children are gifts from Heaven, and mine helped me through many rough roads as I watched them grow."

Hearing Vickie talk about what a blessing children are made my own heart churn. The old wounds were coming closer to the surface, but here in this home, with this peaceful woman before me, it didn't scare me. For now, at least, I wasn't sinking into despair.

"Within a few months of Elisabeth's birth, tragedy hit us like a mighty tidal wave. It was like a double whammy, with my mother ending up in one hospital and Gary in another. You'd better believe I questioned God then. 'How could this all happen at once?' was my question to God.

"First it was my mother. She was flown by helicopter to a hospital in Rockford, Illinois ,in serious condition. She was diagnosed with pneumococcal meningitis, along with a list of other various complications and had slipped into a coma-like state. We were informed that the next forty-eight hours would be crucial for her if she lived. We prayed fervently for her, and played healing tapes declaring she would live.

"Most of our immediate family was from out of state, but when they heard the news, they all came quickly. Since they came so far, most of them ended up staying at my house, which wasn't big enough to accommodate everyone. Some of our family had to sleep on the floor. I didn't think life could possibly get worse, and then, of course, it did.

"Just as I was getting ready to leave for the hospital one morning, there came a knock at the front door. It was my sister-in-law with news that Gary had been in an automobile accident and was in the hospital in Barrington, Illinois. All my plans changed in a moment. I had no idea what Gary's condition was, and all I was told was that I needed to get to the hospital immediately.

"I left my young children behind with the visiting family members. Once I arrived, I learned that Gary had a severe head concussion, along with minor cuts and various bruises. When I went in to see him, he didn't recognize me at first, and couldn't recall who I was. Thank God, this was only for a few moments, but the question remained, just how much of his memory would he recover?

"I was overwhelmed. I felt like I was drowning in tragedy all around me. In the next few days I wouldn't see my children at all. I just went from one hospital to another, relying upon others for transportation since our only car was totaled. With Gary in the hospital, we were without income, out of money, and rapidly running out of food to feed our family and visiting relatives. I was sinking fast.

"In desperation, I went to my home church for aid,

only to be told that they had financial problems and couldn't help us. The only thing I had left to do was to cry out to God, 'HELP!' We were totally dependent upon Him, waiting to see what would happen next.

"And God amazed me. The neighbors on our block took up a collection and deposited groceries on our doorstep. God was providing for us in the midst of the storm.

"From tragedy to triumph, God would get the glory as He intervened. Miraculously, my mother survived three surgeries, including one where her brain was lifted out of her cranium in order to repair a hole in her head. Gary eventually recovered from his injuries and returned to work. I was so grateful to God for all His provision, and I made sure to tell everyone that it was God alone who could have gotten us through that fire."

Something told me that this wasn't the end of this part of the story as Vickie took a moment to think about what she was about to say.

"Everyone went home. As things returned to normalcy in my life, I found myself returning again and again to the fact that in the midst of my troubles, the church, the only organization God Himself had ever set up on earth, had not been there for me. I didn't notice it at the time, but I spent less and less time in my conversations giving credit to God, and more and more time talking about the degree of the trial I had been through. I lost focus on the fact that we had made it through the hardships and had come out alive. I spent less time in prayer and reading God's Word, and as my relationship with God cooled, I began wondering what I had done to deserve all that pain. I started blaming God for all the tragedy, and I grew angry and rebellious towards Him."

Looking at me directly, she said, "You see how I fell

into the enemy's trap? When I stopped seeking God, stopped pressing in to Him, I lost my moorings. The foundation of my life was my relationship with God, and as I rebelled against God, I got caught up thinking about how it seemed so unfair, that life was just cruel. It wasn't long before I stopped spending time at church. Here I was convinced I had been betrayed, and joined ranks with those who would listen to and agree with my rebellious ways.

"As I sank into the miry clay of rebellion, my husband was all too willing to join in my descent. We started going out dancing and drinking as often as possible. That darkness inside of me wasn't eased at all by these activities, but the more time I spent in debauchery, the less the emptiness seemed to hurt."

I identified completely with what Vickie was saying. I hadn't slipped into debauchery to escape the void in my heart; I had immersed myself in my work. My reputation as a reporter came from the relentless hours I spent pursuing the facts of each story I had, no matter what the cost to my "personal life." The fact was that I didn't have a personal life. I had my work, and it took so much attention that I didn't have any left to spare ruminating on my pain, or on the emptiness inside me.

Vickie continued.

"Though I had abandoned God, He had not abandoned me. Instead of punishing me the way I deserved, He sent me a wake-up call. One evening after we had been out dancing and drinking, we were headed home. We were driving along, when suddenly in front of us was a horrible accident. It was pitch dark outside, but I knew black smoke was hanging in the sky. I yelled to Gary, 'Stop the car!'

"That night a drunk driver in a full-size car hit a small car head on, killing those inside. God opened my eyes to the reality of the consequences of our lifestyle. It could just as easily have been us, and where would we be? What would happen to our children without us as living examples for them? We had to make a change in our life and quit rebelling against God; it was hurting us and not Him. The choices I had made were out of pain, but I wasn't punishing God; I was only punishing myself and those around me. I was marred, but I was just adding more to myself by not submitting to the Maker's hand as He fashioned me into a vessel for His purpose."

I found myself wondering how much it would take in her life before she would say "Now I see Your hand, Lord, in the midst of this fiery furnace."

It was easy for me to see the rebellion and its consequences at work in her life, but at the same time, her story was speaking to my own heart. I knew there were many times I had spoken to God without knowledge and in rebellion. I knew that I was a marred vessel. I hadn't yielded to the hand of God, and I was fighting just as hard as Vickie against accepting God's control of my life.

Vickie had seen pain, and joy. She was trying to pass down a legacy to her children. In spite of the horrors she had faced, she wasn't bitter against God. Instead, she had a cultivated peace. I wondered if it was possible for me to get to that point in my own life.

The thought of what it might take to gain that peace horrified me. I wasn't ready to reopen old wounds just to see them heal properly. The last thing I wanted was to bring my shadowed past into the light of day.

Yet Vickie radiated God's love. She was unveiling the love of Christ in a way that I had never seen before.

God had used the tragedy of a drunk-driving accident to pull Vickie closer to Him. Was the tragedy of the fire that brought us together His way of calling me back to Him? She was shining a light into my life, allowing me to begin to see the truth.

Chapter Five

A Time to Reflect

Vickie and I took a break for some lunch. We ate out on her patio, and talked of inconsequential things. The beauty of the day was shining through. The leaves seemed greener than usual, the sky more clearly blue. The golden light of spring shone down on everything.

When we had finished eating, we returned to her living room to continue with her story.

"After seeing the accident, it was like God had thrown a bucket of cold water over me. I had seen firsthand the consequences of living a life of debauchery. When I snapped out of the haze of alcohol and all that partying, I found that Gary and I had slipped into financial difficulties. When you're drinking, your priorities slip, and it's not until you sober up that you realize how much trouble you've gotten yourself into.

"So, I decided to pursue a career in the real estate field. I got my real estate license and studied the business of foreclosure and investment properties. Eventually, I was buying and selling properties, and teaching others about the process of foreclosure on the side. I had become a successful businesswoman, and even learned the ins and outs of the mortgage business. We were digging our way out of the financial hole we had gotten ourselves into.

"True success, though, doesn't come from being able to build a business. Success can only be measured in the degree of your relationships with God and with your family. You can't put anything before God, for it can be easily taken away.

"Trust God even in the midst of raging storms," she said. "For we never know what tomorrow holds.

"One midsummer day, my children were outside playing with friends, and I was working from home. Suddenly, my son came running into the house screaming, 'Julie is dead!'

"You can imagine that he caught my undivided attention. I asked where she was, and what had happened. He told me that an automobile had hit her on her way back from vacation Bible school."

Vickie sighed at this memory. "You know, I was stunned. Julie lived right across the street from us, and she used to help me with the kids. She was an only child, and her parents couldn't have any more children.

"Tragically, it was the truth. She was killed while walking back home from V.B.S. The overwhelming sorrow, grief, and pain that struck her parents had touched us in a way. We reached out, praying for them and encouraging them as best we could. We helped with the funeral services, then watched as Julie's parents grabbed onto the hand of God in the midst of their pain.

"I found myself wondering how I would have reacted if it was one of my children? It was time for me to reflect about this tragic loss and yet see God working in the midst of their situation. God was opening me up to be used by Him as He was now setting the stage, so to speak, for my life.

"Shortly after this tragedy, God began orchestrating a divine plan for us. God was drawing me nearer to Him. I felt like I couldn't drink in enough of His Spirit to satisfy my thirsty soul. Gary and I had heard that the Happy Hunters were coming to Chicago to train healing teams for an upcoming healing crusade. This truly captivated our attention, and so we signed up for their healing school to receive training.

"The last night of the course, we had brought our children. Elisabeth was only three years old at the time, and she told me she saw angels circling the room where the Hunters were giving their service. God was moving greatly, and had laid it on my heart to pray for those in the wheelchair section; however, it took prayer for God to convince my husband this was where He wanted us. Gary finally stood up, volunteering us for the wheelchair section; excitement was building in me, for God was doing a new thing in our lives.

"Once we were in the main auditorium, we were assigned a section. Anticipation was mounting, and we both felt the Spirit of God churning inside us. We knew God was going to move mightily. We felt the Holy Spirit impress us to pray for an older lady in a wheelchair. Going over to her, we stood with Gary right in front of her, and me beside him. We had been instructed to pray in a certain way for healing, but we felt led by the Spirit to simply say, 'In the name of Jesus, rise up.'

"Suddenly she came up out of her wheelchair. God healed that lady that day; she was blind with cataracts, had suffered a stroke, and couldn't walk or talk. God healed everything for her, in an instant; she could see, talk, and walk. We were suddenly surrounded by a group of people who wanted healing or God's touch in their lives too.

"The hand of God healed many that day. One man with a heart problem, another with high blood pressure, a foot problem, and so on; only God knows how many people were healed. Taken down the stairs to the main stage, the older woman shared about her healing, bringing hope and faith to the hearts of many. God

was orchestrating a divine plan as He was setting things into place."

Hearing Vickie talking about these amazing miracles, I was touched at how humble she was about it. Here were people getting up and walking who had been bound to a wheelchair, and she was giving all the glory to God for it, not taking any credit for the healing herself. I admired that about her.

"When I think back to that day," Vickie said, "I realize God was showing a new facet of Himself to me in order to prepare me for what was coming. He wanted me to know exactly how real and how powerful He really is. God wasn't just the God of healing in biblical times; He is the same yesterday, today, and forever. His Word never changes, and neither does He. I was about to learn again how much we, on the other hand, are capable of change.

"Early one evening, the phone rang with horrible news. Two children, both between the ages of two and three, were trapped in a fire and died of smoke inhalation. The children weren't related, and two families had been devastated by the loss. One of the families was friends of my parents, and I had known them distantly when we were growing up.

"The deep agony of loss these two sets of parents suffered was horrible. Two families were devastated. But in my heart, I began to hear the whisper of the Lord saying, 'I came to give life.' I knew then that He was not the one who had taken these two little ones. Satan came to steal, kill, and destroy their lives. Pressing in to God and His everlasting Word, I found deep and abiding trust growing in me. I knew that He has all things in His hands. God was about to take me out into the deep waters of trusting Him, no matter what any man would think.

"Sunday morning, I went to the church where these two families' members attended. There were some believers who believed these children would be raised up to life. God, by His Spirit, was stirring in the hearts of people to believe that He would give life back to these little children. Some people shared visions that God had shown them of these two children being restored to life by God and His Word.

"Over the next couple of days, anticipation grew as a handful of people fasted and prayed, believing for a miracle. God did show up and showed Himself true to His Word, though some didn't see His mighty hand at work. God can work in mysterious ways and not always in ways we can readily see at the time. At His appointed time, He touched one of those little children and brought her back to life long enough for me to witness His awesome power. God doesn't force His people to take His promises or blessings, but those who believe do receive as He promises.

"Unfortunately, the parents of these two children were so overwhelmed with deep sorrow and pain that they missed their blessing, rejecting the gift God intended to give them. Many times we are so overwhelmed with circumstances that we miss the blessing God has prepared for us on the other side. I'm eternally thankful that I got to be one of the witnesses that day, and beheld such a mighty miracle delivered by the hand of God. That day sealed the fact for me that God can raise the dead at any time for those who believe, for nothing is impossible with Him."

Suddenly the reporter side of me piped up, "Is it like when Jesus said, 'Did I not tell you that if you believed, you would see the glory of God?' as it is says in John 11:40? So those who believed saw the glory of God revealed that day."

Quickly she replied , "Yes, and it's also like the story of Jairus' daughter in Mark 6:35-36,when the report was given that his daughter was dead and they told Jairus not to bother Jesus any more. Jesus ignored what they reported and then announced to Jairus, 'Don't be afraid; just believe.'"

Listening to her unfold this story made me wish that I could have been there as one of those witnesses to this miracle. I was wondering now if those children's parents ever realized the miracle they had missed. I wondered how many times I may have missed my own miracle due to the fact my eyes were focused on the vexation that occurred, versus God's delivering hand. She was opening my eyes to seeing how God could use my past to mature me and draw me closer to Him.

"In pursuit of God, I took a trip to Tulsa, Oklahoma, to attend a women's conference. This was one of the first major women's conferences I had ever attended. I could hardly wait to arrive, for I knew God was going to show me something. Excitement was mounting as I registered for the event. I was truly feeling that this would not be like any other service, but more of a building upon the foundation God had already put into my life. God always deposits more of Himself, and this is exactly what He was doing for me. As I look back to that appointed time, I see that I received a great blessing.

"Two beautiful anointed women spoke into my life personally, seeding words of prophecy that would unfold in God's appointed time. I was blessed as Lindsay and Cheryl allowed me into their lives for a short season. There was a bond in the Spirit that God connected between us.

"Lindsay came across the room and said, 'Don't laugh, for one day God will use you, and you'll speak at women's conferences and much more.' Little did she know how terrified I was to speak in front of people back then! Years later, the spoken word became a fact, and I spoke for the first time at a women's conference.

"This first women's conference just increased my hunger, and so I returned for more, each time being blessed by God. God put these anointed women into my life at His appointed time, using them to further me in my journey with Him.

"God positions different people in your pathway for appointed seasons for a divine reason. The Spirit of God was churning within me, drawing me to the realization that we needed to move to Tulsa. The Spirit didn't take long to convince me that we needed to move, but I knew that convincing Gary was going to be something else.

"Then I figured out I wouldn't have to! God had revealed it to me when I visited Tulsa, so I took Gary to Tulsa the next time I went. While we were there, God revealed to Gary that it was His will that we move, and shortly after this visit, we moved as instructed. We had submitted to the fact that God had a plan and purpose for our lives, and for now, at least, it would be found in Tulsa.

Chapter Six

THE JOURNEY BEGINS

I was amazed at the courage it must have taken to pack up and move. The journey of her life had already been filled with great trials, tests, and deep joy. What was it that God had in store for them? How was Tulsa, Oklahoma, going to have an impact upon her and her family?

It reminded me of the story in the book of Genesis where God told Abram to leave his home and go to dwell in the new land where God would lead him. This was the beginning of a new chapter in Vickie's life. However, I was now pondering how could I ever share her story effectively and shed the light of God's hand guiding her through the storms of life.

"Trusting in God, we moved by faith, for there were no employment arrangements made for us. Moving from northern Illinois to Tulsa, Oklahoma, was a great endeavor. Opposition from family members was strong; though knowing God instructed us, we were confident things would work out. Once we arrived in Tulsa, we went to Victory Christian Center where we were warmly received. Victory Christian was expecting us and had arranged for some helpers to help us move into our new place.

"This church wasn't like any other church we had previously attended. The love of Christ demonstrated itself, as people we didn't even know came out of the woodwork to help us. Settling into our new surroundings, we diligently sought for work, which was quite trying some days. However, there was a peace in knowing that God had sent us to Tulsa. Just as our finances dwindled to nothing, and it looked like there was no hope in sight, God came through and blessed Gary with a job. Shortly thereafter I started working at O.R.U. in the correspondence department. It was a time of rejoicing, for God was blessing us spiritually and supplying our financial needs. We started growing in our lives spiritually and did volunteer work at our church.

"Over the next couple of years, we built a home and stayed actively involved at Victory Christian Center. Then the Spirit began stirring within us, pressing us to return to Illinois. At first, we struggled with the idea. We had established a life in Tulsa, and we were growing steadily in the Lord. But you can't fight the changing of the seasons in your life. Once you accept that change has come, God will make it easier for you to make the right decision. He put us in a position where submitting to His plan became easy.

"Financial ruin hit us and we had to file bankruptcy. Devastated by the fact, we realized it was now time to return to Illinois. We thought God might be leading us to start a church in Illinois. We prayerfully considered the matter, and discerned that starting a church wasn't quite what God had in mind for us; He would reveal His plan to us in due time. Settling into our home and acclimating to what God had in store for us was extremely challenging. Change isn't very easy at times for any of us, no matter how necessary it is for spiritual growth.

"God was conducting the whole scene, though at the time I couldn't see the beauty in the midst of the ashes. Trouble was brewing, so to speak. Shortly after we moved back to Illinois, both sides of our families were having a swarm of problems.

"One afternoon, after I had witnessed to my brother and his biker friends, my brother showed up at my door. He asked if he could move in with us for a while, as he had no place to live. I realized that he was in rebellion and angry with God, and was still holding unforgiveness within his heart over past issues. I saw it as an opportunity to witness to him, trusting that God would break forth through his heart once again, and draw him back to Himself.

"Seizing the opportunity to possibly see the tide turn in my brother's life, I asked him to attend a Benny Hinn Crusade in Chicago. The timing was perfect. My brother wanted to give me a birthday gift, and I told him that all I wanted for my birthday was for him to go with me to Benny Hinn's Healing Crusade. Quickly I set him up, praying he would once again recall how God healed me, and somehow realize that God has all things in His mighty hands. He agreed to attend the meeting, and oh, how my heart leaped for joy.

"Yet, even though he went, he wouldn't surrender to the Holy Spirit prompting his hardened heart. I was amazed. How could this be; how could he not see? I was perplexed, and prayed for my brother to return to God. Then the Lord revealed to me that this was the reason He had led us back to Illinois, to help those in need.

"One day as we were driving across town, I noticed a lady with several small children in tow, struggling to walk down the street. I could tell she needed help, and the Spirit prompted me to offer her a ride. We stopped, and it soon became apparent that this was a divine appointment. The woman was one of my high school classmates, Denise.

"Denise remembered me, and asked if I still attended

church. After all these years, she remembered how I had always been ready to give glory to God, and how I talked about what a help it was to have a relationship with Him. You never know how long God will let a seed lie in the earth before bringing it to blossom and grow. God had been working on Denise, and it was time for her to meet up with one of His saints.

"You know, Anne, it's amazing how God brings people together when they're needed most, isn't it?" Vickie said to me.

I had just been thinking the exact same thing, but I still wasn't ready to open up to Vickie. Not yet, anyway, though I was already beginning to think that if God had healed Vickie so miraculously, and brought her through so many trials in peace, then maybe He could deal with that darkness in my past. It just seemed too big, though, and I felt so small.

When I didn't respond, Vickie went on with the story about Denise.

"Denise had just lost a child in a fire. She felt like her life was a field, and had been full of life one day, and reduced to a heap of smoking ash the next. Her face bore the scars of the pain she carried.

"But over the next few months, God allowed seeds of hope to be spread across the field of her life once again. God had brought us together for a season, and used me to bring rays of hope where Denise had seen only darkness and shadow. I was able to take her to church, and she was a witness to God's active, healing love. He used me like the vessel I was to bring Denise healing waters. Of course, you can lead someone to the water, but it's up to them to take the drink." Vickie looked at me meaningfully, and smiled. I laughed, a little nervously, and kind of squirmed in my seat for a moment.

Vickie smiled again, and continued with her life story.

"So, here I was bringing rays of hope into Denise's life. I was so thankful that I had the opportunity to be used by God to help someone, and I wanted Him to use me more. Specifically, I wanted Him to use me to shine rays of hope into my brother's life.

"He was drinking, taking drugs, and running hard away from God. He had known God in his youth, but he had slipped away from God's presence. He wasn't 'tasting of the Lord and seeing that He was good.' His wife had divorced him, and he was angry, bitter at the rejection, and had forsaken God.

"It tore at my heart to see his pain, and I spent long hours in prayer for him. Little did I know that he was about to bring more pain to me and so many others.

"You know, when you're going through a difficult time, you must remember that God permits it for you to grow deeper in Him. He permits difficult times in your life for good, not for evil, and all difficult times pass; He appoints a time for testing, and the time for it to pass. Clinging to this fact can serve as a ray of light, no matter how dark the storms may rage around you.

"Our time of tragedy broke forth like a raging storm; it was a day I'll never forget. We woke to sirens and flashing red lights piercing our bedroom window. I crossed the room to see what the commotion was, and what I saw grieved me deeply.

"A small home on the block behind us had caught on fire. Though the fire was no longer burning, it was evident from the ambulances and other activity that someone had suffered grievous injuries.

"The next morning, we learned that a young girl had been killed, and that the house had been intentionally set ablaze. It was incredible to us; it was almost Christmas. Who could possibly do such a horrible thing, we wondered. We prayed that the Lord would bring the perpetrator of this heinous crime to justice.

"Then, early one morning, the phone rang with news that my parents' house had caught on fire. It occurred near the gas line, though God saw fit that no severe damage was done. However, my parents were both shook up over the incident, and needed help to clean up the mess. We packed up the car with the kids and cleaning supplies and headed over there. Suddenly, a police car was coming up behind us with its siren and lights on, and pulled us over.

"I asked Gary, 'Now what? Were we speeding?' He assured me we weren't, and didn't know why we were being pulled over.

"Shortly, the police officer approached our vehicle and asked Gary to step out of the car. They took him into the patrol car, assured me that Gary had done nothing wrong, and asked that I continue on toward my destination. I had no idea what was going on. I felt like we were in a wagon train, circled up, and that disaster was circling around us.

"I determined to put this aside for now. I chose to focus on what needed to be done at my parents' house, and let God do the worrying. Upon arriving at my parents' home, I quickly organized myself and finished the cleanup that was needed at their home. Feeling compelled within that something just wasn't quite right, I didn't stay to visit.

"The drive home seemed endless. I was assaulted with every kind of frightening thought imaginable. Why did Gary have to leave with the police? They said he didn't do anything wrong, that they just needed to question him. As I turned down the street that led to my home, all my questions were about to be answered.

"Our home was taped off with yellow warning tape

saying 'Do not cross.' Police were walking in and out, going through our possessions. It was like a nightmare.

"I found the police officer in charge, and asked him what was going on. You can only imagine the horror I felt when he told me that my own brother was being arrested for starting the fire that had killed the young girl in the house behind us.

"I didn't want to believe it; I said, 'This isn't possible.' But that didn't change anything. We were forced to realize that my brother was responsible for the death of an innocent young girl. Her parents had to face the tragedy of having their child killed, and we were going through the tragedy of it being my own brother who was responsible.

"The next few months were filled with agony for both sides involved. We were all victims, in our own way. Both of our families were scattered, torn, and overwhelmed with grief, sorrow, and despair.

"Through this time, I turned to the Lord, pressing in to His truth. He gave me a song that brought hope as we passed through this time of shadow. The song was 'Through It All,' and it reminded me that no matter what I faced, God would be with me through it all.

"And God was at work in the midst of our pain. There were times when I had to trust His heart and voice, because I couldn't see His footsteps through the dark shadows of my life. Truly, I could say my soul was overwhelmed with deep sorrow, and quite troubled.

"In the months that lay ahead, God would have to supply us with His strength to make it through. The media, the prosecutor, the people, and even members of our church in Illinois would persecute us. It was time to be 'salted with fire' to see what would come forth. Bold in my commitment to God, I declared that God would see us through this situation. I even witnessed to the prosecution, the media, and anyone who would listen. The Lord let me use this tragedy as an opportunity to share about God, regardless of the present circumstances. God had revealed to me through the previous storms in life to not hide His light in the midst of a raging storm.

"These events impacted many people, changing some for the better, and some for the bitter. My own children felt betrayed by the actions of my brother, and Gary and I took every measure possible to make them feel secure and safe. Witnessing the effect upon each of them at such a young age, I prayed that God would heal their pain, and that they would later see how God used these events to bring strength to them through it all."

As we wrapped up the day's long interview, I found myself wondering if I could ever walk through the fires she had faced and still count it all as a blessing. I had faced fires of my own and at times had failed miserably. I knew that she had experienced struggles, but she also had received strength. Her journey was filled with tests, trials, and tribulation, yet she saw it as developing her character.

As I drove home, I continued to ponder this woman's story, the lessons she had learned, and the message of her life, and wondered how all of these things would affect me. I knew I could not possibly come out of this relationship unchanged.

Chapter Seven

SALTED WITH FIRE

The next day we continued the interview. Vickie began by opening her Bible to the gospel of Mark and showing me verse 9:49, where Jesus says, "Everyone will be salted with fire."

Vickie then began to pick up her story where she had left off the day before. "Let me tell you, I felt well salted while we were going through all the troubles with my brother. God used this time to really bring home to me that He used these fires to purify me, to refine me, to shape me into a vessel He could use. God used these afflictions to bring me to a point of submission to my Maker's hand, and the more He polished and refined me, the more I was able to be used to shine the light of Christ into this dark world.

"The day they sentenced my brother to life in prison without parole, the reality of the situation exploded in me like a bomb. It was a nightmare as I sat in the courtroom hearing the story unfold as the prosecuting attorney represented the evidence of the fire, and the young girl being killed in the process. When they got to the verdict and the sentence, we were shocked. We had been told that the courtroom appearance was in preparation for the trial, not the trial itself. Since we hadn't expected the trial, only my mother and I had come to court.

"I watched the victims as the case was read. Their

pain was written on each feature of their faces. Witnessing the trial was so overwhelming. My mother had a heart condition and high blood pressure; she became my chief concern, especially when the verdict and sentence were pronounced. Mother's knees buckled, and she fell back into her seat weeping.

"I quickly made arrangements with the defender for us to exit the court out the back to avoid the newspaper reporters lined up outside the courtroom. It took only one look from the prosecutor and defender at my mother for them to see that her condition was not good. Swiftly, we were taken out the back to avoid the reporters and my mother was placed safely in the car.

"In the months ahead, this greatly impacted our lives in numerous ways. But God was receiving glory through it all. Even though we stood in the fiery furnace, the fourth Man stood with us. The Son of God was ever present as we faced this fiery trial.

"My parents were hit by the loss of their son in a deep and personal way. They retreated to deal with their own pain, wrestling out their solace with God as they struggled to hold their lives together.

"I was in desperate need of healing myself. I kept hearing the words ringing in my ears: 'sentenced to life in prison without parole.' Everywhere I went, I was reminded that my brother was a convicted felon. Socially, we became outcasts. Although I managed to keep my eyes on God's hand at work through all this, I was one of the few. There were many who would not see God at work in this for a long time, if ever.

"We were wounded, and needed to get somewhere where we could begin to heal. Victory Christian Center had heard the news, and they called us, praying with us for God to direct and comfort us. Shortly thereafter we made the decision to return to Tulsa, Oklahoma, where the healing process would begin.

"We moved in late spring. I knew I was in desperate need of ministry by the hand of God. I was overwhelmed at times by the weight of the pain. Returning to the church at Victory Christian Center felt like coming home, and God began the healing process within me. He showed me that He was directing our steps, and as time passed, the emotional healing took place.

"I remember one evening in particular. We went to the Mabee Center to hear Richard Roberts speak, and God touched us in a very special way. God filled Gary and me with holy laughter as He poured the healing ointment upon us. Truly, we became the center of attraction as we rolled on the floor laughing uncontrollably that evening. The Spirit of God knew what was needed for our healing. Laughter really is the best medicine."

Vickie smiled at me, and I smiled back. I hadn't felt the healing of laughter in a very long time. I yearned for the healing she was talking about, but I just didn't know how to ask her for it.

Vickie continued her story.

"As many different people were placed in our path, God continued to restore and build us from within. Along the way, we came to realize that it was our choice to be healed or to hold on to anger. Slowly we let go of the anger and accepted His ministering love.

"Though I understand that God uses trials and tribulations the way we use salt to season food, I was thankful that He gave us this time of rest from the storms of our lives.

"I was slowly healed. I felt compelled to go into ministry, but I was still caught in a web of deceit from the enemy. He convinced me that due to the scars and mars of my past, I was crippled from effectively ministering to others. Unable to shake the torments of the past, I felt that God couldn't get any glory from my life. I would rather hide those episodes of my felon brother, my unfaithful husband, my sexual assault; the list went on and on. But God is the molder and the maker of my earthen vessel, and He was working out His perfect plan through the ruins of my life, both then and now. God was making me into a vessel that could be used for Him.

"Soon it became apparent that yet another storm was brewing on the horizon of my life. There was a division starting to take place in our marriage. Gary wasn't healed from the past, and anger was mounting within him. He was becoming angrier with everyone around him. Instead of turning to God, he sought to escape the pain he felt inside. He locked me out of his world. He was becoming what is known as a carnal Christian, professing to be a Christian but not showing the fruit of one being submitted to God. It was causing a strong ripple effect upon our marriage. In a desperate attempt to save what I could see was sinking, I confronted him about his anger problem in hopes of awakening him to reality.

"It didn't help. In fact, the problems continued on for a couple of years, and as I felt all hope was lost, I started submerging myself in building a business. I turned to the world to escape my problems, instead of turning to God, and it wasn't long before I started becoming carnal myself, placing things before God. We were still attending church out of duty, and for our children, but deep within I knew that God knew we were not in right standing with Him, and that He was not pleased.

"But God didn't leave me in that position. Many times when His children start to slip out of His hand, God moves in and draws them closer to Him. He didn't let me wander far.

"God started cleaning house, getting rid of the things that I constantly allowed to stand in the way of my relationship with Him. He moved in my life in a way that caused me to sell my business. At the same time, our son got married, and we watched as our oldest left home to embark upon the adventure of married life. He was setting me up, divinely orchestrating the events in my life to draw me into a right relationship with Him.

"The hardest part of the pruning process was yet to come, though. Gary still wasn't dealing with his issues, and avoidance seemed easier for him than confronting the pain still within. The divide between us was deepening, and while I attempted to solve our problems by focusing on God, Gary remained obstinate. He wouldn't let God bring him to humility and brokenness, and it was causing major conflicts in our marriage. It finally became too much for me to handle, and I chose to take action to have Gary removed from the house.

"We were at a crossroads in our lives, and it was time to make a decision. God used this time of separation as a season of growth for both Gary and me. He was shaping us the way that a potter shapes a lump of clay into a vessel that can be used for its intended purpose.

"You know, Anne, to abide within the boundaries of God's law requires complete surrender, a whole submission of our essential self. In our lives, we were stuck in a tug-of-war between the Spirit within and the flesh without. The flesh just doesn't submit without a fight."

I knew that was true. I felt a similar tug-of-war going on in my own heart as I listened to her story, taking notes, and compiling her words. I just couldn't read through what had happened to her without it having an effect on my heart. Through every trial, Vickie had continued to turn more to God, and He kept using her to do more and more for others around her , in spite of the pain she went through.

Vickie went on.

"God was placing us in a position where we would become willing to submit to Him in all things. Looking back, I stand in wonder at how God had His hand on us in the midst of the mess we were in. He really can take a marred, battered old clay pot and make it into a yielded vessel of beauty. Our marriage needed repairs, and there were still more storms over the horizon, as God would need to remold both of us. Determined, I pressed in, seeking God, for He became my burning desire within, I had to know Him more intimately.

"Rebuilding the walls of our broken marriage was difficult. It had suffered damage before, but this time it was different, for I was seeking God, while Gary was floating along like driftwood. He had struggles within that he didn't want to deal with yet. God was once again prompting me to stand by Gary, praying and depositing God's Word within him; and so, determined to be yielded, I did.

"It was during this time that I started hearing God calling me to solitude, where I could be alone with Him, and experience in His presence His direct ministry to my wounds. Whenever I had the chance, I would play worship music, read the Word, pray, study, and talk to God. It was glorious; I was growing by leaps and bounds. It was during this season that God had me write a book. I called it *Dead Men Walking: How to Die to Self* because God was revealing to me how to live the crucified life. This would be essential for me to learn, as God had more trials planned for my sanctification.

"I started praying to be dead to sin, the way Paul describes in Romans 6. The Spirit of God was answering my prayer. I desired to have a heart like Jesus', I would lie on the floor crying out to God that I needed to be more like Jesus. This dying to self was a decision and a process of choosing to die daily; submission to Him in all things became my heart's burning desire. I'm not the only one who missed the fact that Jesus gave all and that we are called to give Him our all. We're told that we were bought at a price. He owns us, having paid for those who believe in Him with His own precious blood.

"The journey was incredible as the Spirit of God taught me, revealing His Word afresh to me. I would spend the evening reading to Gary what God had revealed to me, praying it would heal his pain. I was falling deeper in love with Jesus and couldn't bear to sin against Him or God. God was so real to me, so holy, and I couldn't bear to cause pain to Him who made me. The Spirit of God was doing a work within me, remolding me on the great Potter's wheel. During this time, we sold Gary's motorcycle to pay for my book to be published. God revealed to Gary the importance of having *Dead Men Walking* published.

"God then blessed me with the opportunity to teach others what He had been showing me. Victory Christian Center's women's conference committee asked me to teach a class called "How to Die to Self." The word that Lindsay had spoken into my life earlier was now coming to pass.

"I hadn't spoken or taught for years. I wasn't expecting the Lord to use me in this way at all. This was truly God-ordained; I fasted and prayed, believing God would give me the words when I stood before those ladies at the conference. He didn't let me down at all. God showed up mightily as I spoke on being dead to sin and alive unto God, and the importance of doing it daily. The Spirit of God came in, touching many as they went down under the power of God. It was glorious watching God touch and change people's lives. God gave me the opportunity to speak three times at Victory Christian Center to some of the women, and each time the

Spirit of God showed up, changing lives. God was birthing something new within me for His appointed season.

"But we're never alone in our blessings, and not all those who surround us want to see God's work succeed. The thief was watching the work that God was doing within my family and within my life. God was ready to test me to see if what I had written and spoken about was really ingrained into my heart.

"I had been salted with many tests; laying down my business, giving up my income, and living without enough money to make ends meet. I had submitted in all things, I thought, and then God came to me with the question, 'If I took everything, would you still love Me, or do you love the things and the people around you more than Me?'

"I boldly declared that He was all I needed, not realizing that I would be tested to see if I meant it. Affliction surrounded me once again, this time to see if I would get angry with God or stand firmly on His rock, counting it all joy for Him as He developed me into His yielded vessel."

I shuddered. Vickie had been through so much already, and yet it seemed that there was more to come. Looking back at my own life, I knew that when God had brought His trials and tests, I had failed miserably. I hadn't turned to Him, or even acknowledged Him, yet He was so merciful. Even when Vickie had let herself get distracted by the things of the world, God had been there waiting for her to return to His heart, to His face. I wanted that peace and healing that Vickie had received in His presence, but I still clung to my fears.

Chapter Eight

COUNT IT ALL JOY

Vickie turned in her Bible to James 1:2-4, and read: "Consider it pure joy, my brothers, whenever you face trials of many kinds, because you know that the testing of your faith develops perseverance. Perseverance must finish its work so that you may be mature and complete, not lacking anything."

"Do you see what the trials bring, Anne? God says they bring maturity and completeness. I can honestly admit that at times, this was one of my least favorite passages of scripture. Over the years, though, it has become the most dear to me, because I have lived this passage, I have lived this promise, and God is faithful to His Word. Perseverance had to be developed within me so I could become mature and complete. And perseverance only comes by enduring hardship.

"The Lord took me on a whirlwind journey. I traveled to Florida, Georgia, and Indiana. God was opening doors as I appeared on television three times within a short period of time. My book was selling quickly due to the television appearances.

"I was invited to preach five services at a church up in Omaha, Nebraska, where God did an awesome work at the church. Over ninety percent of the church came to the altar to recommit their lives to Christ. Revival came to that church as they felt the Holy Spirit woo them back to Him. Deliverance from oppression and fear, and miraculous healings, were all taking place by the power of the Spirit of God. Then, right when I was thinking that the Lord was saying 'Charge,' He sounded retreat.

"Personal matters had to be attended to that had not been completely dealt with. My parents' welfare was entrusted to my care. I needed to be there for them. I didn't see how I could take care of them and pursue the Lord's work. I knew that the Bible tells us to take care of our own family first, so I put my ministry in God's hands and returned to take care of my parents. It wasn't long, though, before God provided alternative care for them through my sister. God was still doing His housecleaning. This was all God's divine hand at work. I had already watched as God removed people from within my life that weren't to be a part of my next chapter. God was directing the show, not I. He was in charge. Obedience to Him regardless of the cost was the call, and He rewarded my obedience every time.

"Then the winds of affliction blew in like a hurricane. Gary came to me and confessed that, once again, he had been unfaithful. I remembered thinking after his first infidelity: 'I'll never walk through this trial twice in life.' But God supplied the strength I needed and guided me through the fires of this second affliction. He had warned me in the Spirit that Gary wasn't walking with Him. Betrayed once again, I sat and listened to Gary tell me about his unfaithfulness, but this time it had a different impact on me.

"It didn't hurt me that he had betrayed me personally. God had shown me that it isn't against one another that we ultimately sin, but against Him and Him alone. I was surprised that Gary didn't see that he was being unfaithful to God, to his commitment to Him. His betrayal wasn't just to me; he was betraying his covenant with God.

"But Anne, you have to realize that dealing with severe financial hardship, my parents' issues, my husband's betrayal, and the pain that caused my children became more than I could bear all at once. While I recognized God was at work in my trials, I desperately needed to be in His presence to keep from getting swept away in the storm and from losing my focus on God. I left to be alone with God, and prayed earnestly seeking His guidance. Although in my spirit I could count it all joy and laugh at the devil's tactics, I still felt overwhelmed in my soul. I had to cling to the towers of truth He had given me as the winds tore at my heart and mind.

"God told me very clearly that I needed to pour what He had given me into Gary. By His grace, I chose to forgive Gary. All I wanted was to show him how much God loved him. It's only in learning God's love that we can find our way to repentance. God helped me to persevere, and when I felt in my soul like giving up, I turned instead to the Lord, casting my cares, fears, and pain on Him, and I managed to stay steadfast with Him through this trial.

"I realized that God was shaking or removing everything in my life that I had ever put my trust in other than Him. God had requested my business, so there was none, and then my ministry, and then He had given me great financial despair. He had removed people from our lives, and then He took us from our home church.

"God had asked me before, 'Would you be willing to give up all for Me?' I had declared before God that He was all I needed. I had written my book about dying to self, and now I was truly being tested in that. Yielded to God in all things, I sought His will as my highest priority. God was everything to me; I loved Him with all my heart, soul, and mind, with every ounce of my being. Total commitment to Him took first place in my life; no other thing came before my God. If the flames of affliction were what I had to walk through to be more refined and to shine more with the love of Christ, then so be it."

Vickie sighed then. She sighed the way adults sigh when they think back on the foolishness of their own childhood rebellion. I was moved by her commitment to and obvious love for God. She had let go of everything that was important to her.

There were many times in my own life that I had grown frustrated with God's expectation that we should put everything in His invisible hands. I wondered how she could endure so much. She had been betrayed not once, but twice, was in financial ruin, was no longer ministering, was helping her children with their pain, and was coping with the loss she had suffered. Yet still, when she spoke of her love for Christ, her face shone. She was truly devoted to Him. He was the source of her strength; she was walking through the flames of life holding on to Him in all things. Through it all she had learned to trust in Jesus and learned to put her faith in God.

Horrible things had happened to Vickie, and Vickie clearly had admitted that she had turned away from God because of them. Yet still, He called her back, loved her, forgave her, and granted her the strength and peace to face the hardships that were so common in life. What about me? Would God forgive me? Was He calling me back to Him through this woman's life story? Was it possible for me to be healed from my sins of the past, and to be able to talk so candidly about them without shame or regret?

Vickie went on, and as she spoke, I felt her speaking God's wisdom into my darkened heart.

"God is a God of restoration, for He rebuilds broken

lives. Gary was being broken, brought to a place of submission to God. I was being tried in the fire, to see if I would choose to love unconditionally and pray for restoration. Praying was easy for me; I had learned how to pray without ceasing. The Spirit of God had taught me how to pray in my spirit man."

I interrupted, "What is that, the spirit man?"

"The Bible talks about how we have two sides of us, the 'old man' and the 'spirit man.' The spirit man longs to be obedient to our loving Father in Heaven, while the old man struggles to pursue sin. Even after we're saved, the old man can sneak his way of thinking into our lives, and the Bible exhorts us to put off the old man and to put on the spirit man, to walk in the Spirit. When I was praying in my spirit man, I was praying the prayers that God wanted me to pray, not what my flesh wanted. I didn't pray for the Lord to take away my pain and make everything perfect. I emulated Christ in the Garden of Gethsemane, praying, 'Lord, if it's Your will, take this cup from me; but nevertheless, not my will but Yours be done.'

"It was tough, at times. I was worried about repercussions Gary's betrayal would have on our children. I didn't want this to hurt their trust in God. But that, too, I resigned to God's hands. I had done the best I could to train them in the way they should go, and now that they were adults, it was up to them to seek the Lord. God doesn't have any grandchildren. So I kept them in my prayers, trusting in God to mold and make them into the vessels He intended.

"Elisabeth, our youngest, was to be married shortly, and her wedding was approaching quickly. We had promised her that she would have a beautiful wedding, everything just as she had planned.

"Meanwhile, God was rebuilding our fractured marriage, this time stronger than ever before. For Gary was a new man in Christ, walking in love, joy, peace and being a witness testifying to others the power of God. God had brought a special friend into my life. Her name was Pam, and she was a mighty prayer warrior. She helped me walk through this season of my life. She was always there to take time to pray with me, to listen to me when I had to talk about what was going on, and to give me words of encouragement. Pam imparted to me God's words of life in a difficult time.

"I shared with Pam how God had given me a vision years ago, of walking through the fire but never being burned or harmed. It was a raging fire with rubble falling all around me, but God kept me safe through it all.

"With Pam's help, we discerned that God was calling me to give hope to those passing through the fires of affliction. Everyone is salted with fire; everyone is tested and tried. God wanted me to bring hope to those in the midst of struggle, and to point the way to Him, to the only One who can give us the strength to face the fires, and to be healed from our past.

"Seeking God in all things, submitting to the Maker, had become my life's main objective. God took control of our marriage and rebuilt it. He brought us to a small church where He was about to reveal the next stage of His plan for us. We still had to deal with financial difficulties and our children's spiritual growth, but we had learned that waiting on God is the only way to get anything done right. We had learned that He is in control and uses all the trials and tests to bring His children into submission to Him, where He can use us. We were counting it all joy, watching as God moved."

Chapter Nine

Through It All

Vickie's story was having a tremendous impact in my heart. Through it all, she had learned to trust in Jesus and had confidence in God. She was opening my eyes to the fact that Satan was holding me in bondage over my past, preventing me from ministering effectively to those in need. I saw how she had been delivered from her shame of the past, and how God had used her to become a witness for Christ Jesus to those around her. She had been deceived into believing that her past held her in captivity. Her words were giving me hope, hope that I too could be healed from the mars of my past. She was shedding the light of God's truth into the shadowy darkness of my soul.

Crossing the room, she picked up the book she had written, *Dead Men Walking*, and proceeded to read the following poem to me.

> Valley of Broken Pieces
> *by Carol Mickelson*
>
> *My spirit was high,*
> *My life a song,*
> *My heart was proud,*
> *My will was strong.*
> *Then one day came the voice of Jesus,*
> *And I saw a valley of broken pieces.*

As an eagle I soared, untouched and high.
I'd rather have stayed up there in the sky.
But quietly called the voice of Jesus:
"Come to the Valley of Broken Pieces."
Down I swooped, and was filled with awe
at the beautiful, fearful things I saw!
Yet come the comforting words of Jesus:
"I'm here in the Valley of Broken Pieces.
Brokenness is the best gift I give.
I ask you to die, that others may live.
It's your choice,"
challenged the voice of Jesus.
"Rest in the Valley of Broken Pieces.
Lo, I am with you; have no fear.
I'll teach you to love, and bring others cheer.
Forgiveness is yours," assured my Jesus,
"Only in the Valley of Broken Pieces."
I went to the valley, and saw the "I."
I saw the pride, which had to die.
I found new freedom—release—in Jesus,
And wholeness now, instead of pieces!
Once I thought "I" could do it all.
Now at my Savior's feet I fall.
I'm just a vessel, to be filled with Jesus,
which He created from broken pieces.
Yes, I was broken so I might be healed.
When self was strong, Christ was concealed.
Now through me shines the light of Jesus.
Oh, blessed Valley of Broken Pieces!

Vickie looked back up at me with light shining in her eyes. "Anne, can you see how the light of Christ now shines through my broken past, displaying that God can and desires to heal and restore shattered lives? It took me choosing to be submitted to God; it took me crawling up on His altar as He broke apart those things that had become idols in my heart before Him. My circumstances had been a raging fire at times; there were fearful things He called me to walk through as He molded my character to become more of a reflection of Him. Though I heard His voice comforting me, I was there in the Valley of Broken Pieces. God delights in taking marred vessels within His mighty hands and molding them into yielded vessels fit for His divine purpose.

"God had placed us in a little church that wasn't quite what we had expected, but we had learned that submission to Him is obedience. In the midst of our obedience, He revealed blessings to us and to those He brought into our lives. At this church, we found a story waiting to be written. God had a little lady sitting in that church who had lived a life of great sorrow, loss, defeat, and utter pain. She had a smile, but beneath it one could see the tears from her pain. It happened one Sunday morning as God unfolded a portion of her life before the congregation. The song 'Through It All' had been played. This song broke within her spirit as God reached down from Heaven, touching her especially through the line 'I've learned to trust in Jesus.'

"She walked the aisle to the altar to share her story. Sobbing, she managed to get the words out: She had lost her son. She had just returned from witnessing the trial and verdict of the young man who had killed her son.

"It was evident to us that God was conducting this service as this woman told how her son had died in her arms, stabbed to death. Then she expressed how she sat in court as the young man who committed the crime requested her forgiveness; this was difficult, but she forgave him. Then he asked her if God would forgive him. She replied that God would forgive him, but that he needed to ask God himself.

"God was in control as He always is, even in the midst of tragedy; there comes triumph to those who persevere. He had brought this sweet lady to the service to be ministered to, even as He had used her to bring the Gospel message to the murderer of her own son.

"God had placed me and Gary in this service, for such a time as this. We had been down that long, dark road, and we were able to minister peace to this lady. The Spirit of God prompted me to pray over her, breaking the yoke of bondage from the pain and sorrow she had suffered. Truly God knew just what this lady needed, and at the same time, God brought me to share the story of victory He had wrought in my own life regarding my brother.

"Orchestrating is God's specialty; He molds, makes, and redesigns us upon the Potter's wheel through it all. This was God's appointed time to touch this lady's life, and we were well acquainted with the sorrow, grief, and despair that surrounded a situation like this. We were also aware of how these situations can draw you closer to God, forcing you to become completely dependent on Him as He guides and protects you in the midst of the flames. He poured out the oil of healing upon her life; it would only be the first application of the oil, for there was more to come.

"Within the next couple of weeks, I arranged to meet with this lady. God was to receive the glory, as He would take the ashes of her past and turn it into triumph. I was looking forward to hearing her life story. Truly this sweet little lady had been through some great trials, as she had lost both of her sons. How could one bear to lose their only two children in life? She had suffered the pains of divorce, the loss of her first child in a car accident, and now the loss of her second child by murder.

"The only way through so much devastation is to call on God. She had witnessed the murder of her second son, and she had held him as he drew his last breath in her arms. She had cried out to God, 'No, not my last child!' Her pain was evident, but even as she spoke, the healing ointment was being applied to her pain. God had a plan, and through it all she would put her trust in God. Shortly after the loss of her younger son, this little lady became ill to the point of death, with double pneumonia and a spot on her lung. But God had a plan for her, and He healed and restored her. Her destiny in life was still being written; she had a message to share with others.

"God is with you even in the midst of great tragedy and will turn your sorrow into joy. God was rebuilding His strength within her, His compassion, and drawing her closer to Him."

I was moved by the story Vickie told me. God had used her own fiery trial to prepare her to minister to another of His children in her time of need. This stirred up questions in me, questions that had nothing to do with getting the story.

"Vickie, why does God test us," I asked. "It doesn't make sense."

Vickie smiled and said, "That's tomorrow's lesson."

I knew that our conversation for today was over, and I also knew her stopping the story where she did was intentional. I spent my evening contemplating my own question, trying to resolve it with my own intellect. Try as I might, I could not reason it out on my own. My efforts dried up and I knew I could only wait to get the answers from her in the morning.

Chapter Ten

GOD TESTED US

I was impatient for her to start as I sat watching her put the kettle on to make tea. I knew her reason for making me wait until morning to get an answer to my question—I had concluded that I could not answer it in my own strength or reasoning. Now she would give me the answer from the Word of God, the only place I could turn to, now that I had exhausted my own human logic.

Once we were settled comfortably at the kitchen table with hot tea and the recorder running, she began once again.

"In Genesis 22:1, the Bible says, 'Some time later God tested Abraham.' Then Hebrews 11:17 states, 'By faith Abraham, when God tested him, offered Isaac as a sacrifice.'

"God will test us in order to prove our commitment to Him. Establishing the difference between being tested and being tempted is essential here. You see, testing comes from God, but temptation comes from Satan. Test means to examine or evaluate what is in one's heart. The book of James tells us in 1:13-14, 'When tempted, no one should say, "God is tempting me." For God cannot be tempted by evil, nor does He tempt anyone; but each one is tempted when, by his own evil desire, he is dragged away and enticed.'

"Satan tempts us with evil desires in order to make

us fall. The purpose of Satan's tempting us is to drag us away from God. God's tests are to evaluate or examine our heart, for God's tests strengthen our character to be more like Him. God's Word promises that He will never give us more than we can bear. His tests are to teach us to turn to Him and trust in Him. We all experience temptation, and we all experience times of testing. And sometimes, when someone we know and love falls into temptation, it brings to us a time of testing. God permits our hearts to be examined to show forth what is in us.

"Even Jesus was tempted, and you can read about this in Matthew 4:1: 'Then Jesus was led by the Spirit into the desert to be tempted by the devil.' While there, He was tempted 'in every way, just as we are—yet without sin,' as it states in Hebrews 4:15. Christ's temptations never led Him to sin; Jesus defeated Satan by using the sword of the Spirit. Jesus, the perfect role model, demonstrated to us how to fight the war against Satan. He showed us that totally submitting to the Spirit of God and standing firm in the Word of God proves our commitment to God when being tempted. When we use the Word as our weapon of defense, it sends Satan fleeing.

"I hope this revelation of the difference between being tested and being tempted helps you, Anne. When you're feeling overwhelming pressure in your spirit over a particular trial, cry out for help from the One who is acquainted with sorrow and pain and endured temptation, our Lord Jesus Christ. We don't need to walk through the darkness alone if we hold onto the hand of our Deliverer.

I brought her back to my question of yesterday. "But why do we need to be tested?" I asked Vickie.

"There are passages throughout Scripture that reveal

why we all need to be tested. In Deuteronomy 8:2 and Mark 9:49, the Bible says, 'Remember how the LORD your God led you all the way in the desert these forty years, to humble you and to test you in order to know what was in your heart, whether or not you would keep his commands.' 'Everyone will be salted with fire.' Then in Malachi 3:2, we read, 'For he will be like a refiner's fire or a launderer's soap.' Both fire and soap are used to eliminate impurities. God tests us to remove things from our lives that shouldn't be there.

"It was difficult at times in my life to submit to the tests and trials. I admit that at times I failed the test miserably, and needed to be refined in my character. But lately, I've grown to yearn after being more like Christ Jesus and having a heart like His. I grew weary of quarreling with my Maker over the work of His hands in molding me. I resigned myself to the fact that I wouldn't give orders to God about the work of His hands in molding me in the fires to complete my character. God knew what He needed to do to mold me into a vessel fit for His use, and I wasn't ashamed of my past. I've learned to wear it as a badge of honor. The work God has done in my life gives glory to Him and shows others that they can have the same peace that I now have.

"All through God's Word you will find people who needed to be molded. Peter denied Jesus three times before the rooster crowed. Not only Peter, but all the disciples deserted him and fled, as stated in Matthew 26:56."

Turning in her Bible to Luke 22, she read to me the passage where Satan asked to sift Peter as wheat, but Jesus prayed for Peter so that his faith would not fail, and so that when Peter would turn back and repent, he would strengthen his brothers.

"Do you see," she asked, "that being tested refines a person? Passing the test is the goal, but we often fail. When we do, we shouldn't be disheartened. It is in our failures that we gain enough experience and strength to encourage and strengthen others.

"At first as we examine ourselves, we think we can never become what God wants. Wrong, wrong, wrong!" she exclaimed. "We don't need to be ashamed of our past. Paul wasn't, Peter wasn't, King David wasn't, Mary Magdalene wasn't, so why are we? The Bible is full of examples of others who were delivered from and learning from their past. From their failures, they grew in their faith enough to begin sharing it with others. Learning to submit to God in all things is living a life of absolute surrender to Him. Peter used the lessons he learned from his failures to strengthen others. King David, a man after God's own heart, repented after sinning with Bathsheba and having Uriah killed."

I could see her message unfolding before me. My own past wasn't something to be ashamed of; I could take my failures and give them to God. Then He could use them to His glory by showing me how to use my past to help others.

Questions were mounting in me. My mind was swirling with all that she had said; yes, I could learn from those in the Bible who hadn't hidden from their past. I finally understood the part of being tested by God and tempted by Satan, and how I had been given the right to choose. I felt like this interview process was a test in itself for me. I needed time to process it all, so I suggested that it was time for me to call it a day once again and contemplate what we had talked about.

Driving home, a light rain was once again falling. I was replaying her words through my mind. So much had been said, and though I had the answer to yesterday's question, more questions were coming to me. I didn't understand how all of what was said could fit together, let alone deliver me. I had to read the book she had written; maybe then I would see something I missed before. Interviewing her was different from any other interview I had ever done; she was making me examine things I had never wanted to look at again.

Chapter Eleven

THE MINGLED LIFE

The next day, I went to her home again. I had written out my questions for her, no longer for the purpose of getting the story, but to help me understand what God was doing in my life through our interaction.

She was waiting for me as if she knew the very questions that were circling in my mind.

"Anne, today we're going to talk about something different, something the Lord has shown me, and I think some of your questions will be answered.

"See, in the covenant relationship, there are two parties involved: God and man. Man's part calls for faith and 'surrendership,' a yielding of himself to God's work and will within his life.

"Let's examine the story of Ishmael and Isaac, the two sons of Abraham. Ishmael was born a slave; Isaac was born free. Ishmael was born after the flesh and by the will of man; Isaac was born through the promise and the power of God. Their births represent very well how one can be led astray when trust is misplaced in the flesh. This story of the conception and birth of these two sons of Abraham represents two ways of living: in bondage and in freedom.

"You'll find that these two ways of living exist in the Church today. There are two stages, or classes, of Christians in today's Church—two ways in which Christians serve God. The first is from the religious or elementary level, and the second is from the more advanced, spiritual, seeking level. Some are content living the mingled life, half flesh and half spirit, half self-willed and half submitted to God's will. Others seek to submit their whole beings to God, knowing what He meant when He said 'dead to sin and alive unto God.' This group seeks to abide in the fullness of God, empowered by His Holy Spirit for His purposes. They desire to be imitators of Christ, reflections of Jesus' love to those around them.

"Do you ask yourself if it's really possible to become dead to sin amid the daily struggles in life? Rather than analyze such a question, ask yourself, 'Is God a God who never changes and isn't His Word true?' He can't change His Word. It is forever established. His covenant with us is clear. It's our part that gets misunderstood. If we believe, in faith, submitting our entire being up to Him daily, we die to sin and become alive in God. One of my favorite songs is 'I Surrender All.' The 'All' in that title means all of oneself.

"Past failure taught me one important thing: I was an unsurrendered soul. The carnal part, the flesh, wanted to rule rather than fully submit. God calls us to lay down our lives for Him. That's how I came to write my book. I prayed over and over again, 'Lord, give me a heart like Jesus', willing to walk in obedience, love, and surrendership to You. Lord, grieve my heart if I grieve Your Holy Spirit.' Continually I asked for a heart like Jesus'. Through this, God revealed His Word to me, changing me by His Spirit. This was how my soul became surrendered to Him."

Her words contained so much love and adoration for Jesus that they melted me. Each word resounded in my ears, "Oh, I love Him more than anything, anyone, and even more than life itself." She lit up as she expressed how she loved Him.

"And what's more, through His love you can forgive anyone and stand praying, believing God to deliver them from the hands of the enemy. With God nothing is impossible, and with His love dwelling in you, the mingled life ceases to exist."

I was in awe of what God had accomplished in her life so far. There was no bitterness, resentment, or anger, but rather hope, love, and peace. She had opened something within me which had been held captive through deep sorrow, rejection, and loss. Her life was revealing to me how to love, forgive, and stand believing even in the midst of the storms of life. I could feel my spirit being pulled by the hand of God to surrender into His hands—His Spirit wanted to mend the marred places of my own entangled life.

She opened her Bible to read from 1 Corinthians chapter 13. "God will show us the most excellent way. 'If I speak in the tongues of men and angels, but have not love, I am only a resounding gong or a clanging cymbal [merely making noise]. If I have the gift of prophecy and can fathom all mysteries and all knowledge, and if I have a faith that can move mountains, but have not love, I am nothing. If I give all I possess to the poor and surrender my body to the flames, but have not love, I gain nothing.' So therefore the greatest of all these things is love.

"Anne, being tried in the fires of affliction taught me surrendership, or obedience, to Him: submission of body, soul, and spirit. But the greatest gift was His love that now floods my life and also my husband's life."

I believed her; the love she displayed was changing peoples' lives, including mine.

I had never heard anyone pour out their life in such a way as she had, and she was wanting me to see that Jesus was molding me and could take marred vessels and mold them into vessels to be used for His glory. I was beginning to feel broken and could hear the voice of Jesus, beckoning to me to come to the Valley of Broken Pieces. I was ready to submit to His will and plan for my life; after all, I had made a mess by trying to mold myself instead of allowing Him to make me.

She had shared the greatest gift, the gift of love, and how genuine love can transform marred vessels into yielded vessels. There was no pretense here, for her life was a display of her love towards others, and she had certainly displayed it to me.

"Anne, the greatest sign of spiritual maturity is to possess a heart of love, to love one another with a pure heart fervently. For anyone to speak the right things or say the right words, to have the gift of prophecy, the gift of healing, or any of the other gifts does no good unless you've been immersed in the depths of Christ's genuine love."

My heart was pounding so loud in my chest, I was certain she could hear it and surely see that I needed this genuine love to transform me. How could it be that she walked through the fires of life and was infused with such a heart of love through it all? No bitterness, anger, resentment, or shame remained in her life, only a peace, love, and joy. I was desperate for that love of Christ to heal my own marred past, to remove the shame, anger, and bitterness. She had the answer that I had been searching for; brokenness was the answer, for from my brokenness I would finally surrender to the Maker, allowing His love to flood my soul. Suddenly it was as if everything that had been dammed up broke loose. I began to weep uncontrollably.

Quickly she reached out to me, holding me, telling me that God was present to touch me and heal me. She ministered to me in genuine love with a heart full of compassion. When my tears were finally spent and we reached a place of peace, I took my leave of her and returned to my own home. I knew that a new stage was unfolding in my life.

Chapter Twelve

THE GREATEST GIFT

The light of a new day was dawning; I felt refreshed and bathed in the waters of God's unfailing love. I was supposed to be interviewing her, but somehow it turned out that she had uncovered a story hidden within me. Oh, it didn't matter, for it was glorious. I was liberated at last, and I wanted to just thank the Lord all day long. The greatest gift of all was now being unfolded in my heart and life, the gift of His love.

God brought me to the place of brokenness of spirit. He was remolding me, making me into a yielded vessel to be used for His divine will in life. God was turning my weakness into a testimony of strength, all to His glory. My heart had only one attraction, only one true love. His love penetrated the depths of my heart and shone a light in it that I never saw before. I was now prepared to yield to His call and to His desires for my life.

As Vickie had shared His Word the day before, it had become alive within me. She had talked the day before about being united in Christ, having the same attitude, tenderness, compassion, humility, and purpose. She had demonstrated to me His attitude of self-sacrificing humility and genuine love for others. She was not looking to her own self but to the interest of others being made whole in mind, body, soul, and spirit.

Excitement was building as I anticipated finishing

my interview with her. I could hardly wait to arrive at her home, knowing God had more to reveal to me. God was truly showing me the most excellent way in which to walk and live, and that was all in His love. As I approached her house I could hear music playing.

The song playing as I entered was *Change My Heart, O God*, written by Eddie Espinosa. The lyrics were perfect and so fitting. It was ministering to my spirit.

Change my heart, O God,
Make it ever true.
Change my heart, O God,
May I be like You.
You are the Potter,
I am the clay;
Mold me and make me,
This is what I pray.
Change my heart, O God,
Make it ever true.
Change my heart, O God,
May I be like You.

Vickie welcomed me into her home. When we were situated, Vickie began.

"Anne, there is a secret place in Jesus that one can dwell in. So many of us have been weighed down and almost crushed with troubles. Many of us thought we would never get out of this place of difficulty, but behind it all, God has been working a plan greater than the troubles we've known. God wants us to come to the end of ourselves and, by the power of His love, rise up into a life where He rules and reigns.

"With a heart full of God's compassion, we will help those who carry heavy burdens and set them free. The greatest gift is the gift of love—a heart full of compassion moved to see the captives set free. Love is a heart that won't quit praying for, standing for, believing in, and speaking life into an individual who has a broken heart. To be like Jesus, we should encourage a transformation to occur in others so they will live and move in the atmosphere of holiness.

"In John 13:34-35, Jesus emphasized this new commandment that He left with us. 'A new command I give you: Love one another. As I have loved you, so you must love one another. By this all men will know that you are my disciples, if you love one another.' Love is the distinguishing mark of Christ's followers; it is Christ's love for us flowing out of us to those around us. God is the one who can perfect the imperfect by His own loving touch.

"It is a blessed thing when the old vessel becomes broken for the glory of God, for God has a way of reshaping and molding vessels anew."

"God had chosen me to go through certain experiences to profit others. Throughout history, God has had His witnesses as He would chasten, correct, mold, teach, and move them in order to refine them to meet the needs of some needy soul who would otherwise go down without such comfort and love. All the chastening, correction, and hardship is worth it, for His Spirit strengthens us so that we may endure and bring comfort and compassion to others in need.

"We read this in 2 Corinthians 1:3-4: 'Praise be to the God and Father of our Lord Jesus Christ, the Father of compassion and the God of all comfort, who comforts us in all our troubles, so that we can comfort those in any trouble with the comfort we ourselves have received from God.'"

The words she spoke brought light and comfort to me. She understood my pain and wanted me to see that

Jesus loved me and would heal my past scars, using them all for His glory. I was no longer ashamed of my past; after all, if I hid my past, how could I help or understand others who were in need? Compassion was growing in my heart; it was flooding my soul. She showed me that God wants us to have a pure love, a love that always helps someone else at its own expense. Exposing my own hurts to help others sounded like an enormous step of faith to me. I was just beginning to experience my own healing. Was I ready to step out into helping others?

Chapter Thirteen

SURRENDERED LIVES

"What is obedience?" Vickie asked. "Is it not surrendership to God, to do as He commands? Obedience is to do the will of the Father; it's living the submitted, yielded life of abiding in Him."

These words she was speaking were truth; she was bearing the fruits of His Spirit within her life to those around her.

I wanted to continue with the story of the journey of her life. She rested back as she began.

"God will send you to places for a season, or even to a person or two. Communicating with the Father to obtain your instructions is important. Time had passed and God had us leave the little church where the little lady who had suffered the loss of her children attended. God would do a work in this little lady by His Spirit and send others to sow in her life.

"God impressed me to hold another conference. I invited an anointed speaker named David. He wasn't well known, but he walked in love, and had the fruits of the Spirit operating in him along with the gifts of prophecy and healing. We had a beautiful service; God really showed up, touching and changing lives all for His glory. Gary and I both felt that God had brought David and his ministry to us.

"God was also burning within Gary and me to start holding weekly services. So we rented a small building for a couple of months in which to hold services. God moved in the services. It was in this season that Gary moved forward to a new level of faith. He finally surrendered to the Spirit of God to preach the Word, sharing from his heart. I had always been the one who preached before, but God revealed by His Spirit that Gary could share the Word also. Our excitement mounted as God performed a new work in us and unfolded His plan for us as a couple. We had seen healings and deliverances, and had received spoken words of prophecy over us. Now we were facing a new season.

"There was a new page turning in our lives. God was positioning us both to do His work, together, for His glory. Our disposition and character reflected what was within us: The love of Christ had flooded our hearts. The blessed path we were walking in was divine love expressed by the emptying of ourselves and the sacrifice of our wills to God's will. We were truly abiding in Christ's love, seeing the fruits of the Spirit manifesting in us, and helping others to walk in closer union with the Lord. I had traveled, speaking as an evangelist, but God was calling us to do a new thing together. I knew God would still continue to use me as an evangelist, but He was positioning us as a couple to do even more for Him."

Vickie said, "I was content to wait and see what God would reveal to us in the coming year. My spirit was still and in peace, waiting upon God for His instructions."

Vickie's pause gave me time for reflection. God had positioned me here, at this time, in this place, so she could help me see more of Him and recommit myself into His hands, to mold me as He would see fit. Even now, He was launching me into the waters of a new way of living, the life of absolute surrender and peace.

Vickie 's voice broke through my quiet reverie as

though she had been reading my mind. Quietly she spoke the following poem.

Every second, I choose to be
kept by Christ's love.
Every second, I choose to receive
life from above.
Every second, I choose to abide
in the Vine.
Every second, I choose to yield
to His will.
Crucifying self, God's glory
is revealed.
God of perfect love, reflect
Thy love through me.

"I wrote that myself," she confessed to me. "I knew the cost of being submitted and the importance of waiting for His instructions. Walking with Jesus is walking according to His divine example just as He illustrated to all of mankind, to stay in tune with God. Now I try to abide in Christ. He is the vine, and I'm merely a branch bearing forth His fruit through me. My purpose is to serve, bear forth His fruit, and love one another. The reason for my existence here on earth is to bear forth His fruit."

Her childlike spirit illustrated to me the importance of abiding in Him and seeking every moment of that life from above. Those who abide in Him...bear much fruit.

I wanted to bear that fruit too. I no longer felt hindered from triumphing over the obstacles of my past. Christ's love was so infinite, intense, and divine; the Holy Spirit conquered my marred past, shedding His light and revealing God's glory.

"What about you, Anne?" Vickie asked, startling me out of my thoughts. "Are you ready to share your past, and be freed from your own bondage?"

I was filled with warmth from my head to my toes, and I felt a calm joy come over me. The journey of my life had really just begun, for I was no longer ashamed of my past history. I saw my life as a retuned instrument that could be used for the good of others now. I now found myself excited to share things that had previously frightened me to reveal. God had done a work in my heart by removing the guilt, shame, and despair of my past. For the first time, I could see all the negatives in my life becoming a positive as the light of Christ shined in on them.

Deep down, I had wanted this opportunity to unload the things I had hidden inside of myself, but I hadn't known how to ask. Thanking God, I opened up to her and told my own story.

Chapter Fourteen

A Changed Heart

Traveling back through the pages of my own life, I now shared my own story with a heart full of peace. I had grown up in a Christian home, but had never really developed a serious relationship with the Lord. My family's faith was very superficial. We lived one way on Sunday morning and just like everybody else the rest of the week. I knew all of the Bible stories but had never made the connection that their lessons applied to me. Consequently, when I reached college, my lack of roots in the Word caused me to drift into living the life of the worldly.

My real heartaches seemed to start with the episode of my affair. I had taken an internship over the summer between my sophomore and junior years. There at my workplace I met a man who was charming, attractive, and eager to serve as my mentor. Eventually I fell into a relationship with this man. Unfortunately, he was a married man who had children. At the time I didn't care about that. I saw him through selfish eyes as a step up the ladder of success. He saw me as a mild fling. During this affair, I became pregnant by him. When he found out, he broke off our relationship right away. Suddenly faced with the harsh reality of my situation, I chose to have an abortion.

The decision was made quickly and without a second thought. I didn't have a relationship with Jesus. This pregnancy and child simply didn't fit in with the life that I wanted at this point in time. I was still in college, and obtaining my degree was most important to me then. I got the abortion, but hadn't counted on the intense grief and guilt that would follow.

As I spoke, I felt peace for the first time. I had always felt such shame and guilt. Now, God had truly touched the shattered pieces of my heart with His healing hand of love. The pain and shame of the abortion had been lifted from my marred past. I was able to go on with my story without experiencing the pain and remorse I once had.

Once I finished college and got my degree, I started looking for a job in journalism. I faced many obstacles even then, so as I endeavored to fight off depression, I turned to using drugs to keep me more upbeat. It seemed like I found an upside to my life then, at least for a while. I started losing weight, and my abundance of energy made me work harder and eat less. Needless to say, it caught up with me.

I had an opportunity for a great job, but I'd have to pass the physical exam first. I figured I would just go off the drugs and reschedule my exam for later. It was the best way to land the job.

The next few weeks turned out to be miserable. I had gotten addicted to the drugs, and the withdrawal racked my body with pain. I knew now that God must have been with me, for I made it through.

I did land the job and made a name for myself, so to speak. Life was looking good; I soon developed a serious relationship with a young man named Guy, and we began to plan for a future together. Things couldn't have looked better for me. We bought a townhouse and moved in together. We were planning on being married. A couple of months after moving into the townhouse, I found out I was pregnant again, and this time I wanted to keep the child. Guy was a good man; he had been raised in church and treated me very well.

Guy wanted a church wedding, and insisted we start attending church. It wasn't long after attending his church that the pastor brought in a guest speaker who touched our lives. We made a decision that day to give our hearts to Jesus, and to no longer live together until we were married. Guy let me live in the townhouse and he rented a small apartment.

The wedding was only weeks away and I still wasn't showing with child yet. But the darkest day of my life dawned abruptly, suddenly changing my world. I could recall that day perfectly. Guy was driving home from a late night at work. He was traveling on a poorly lit street, and a drunk driver hit him head-on. Guy didn't make it; he died instantly, leaving me behind. The news was more than I could bear. In my horror, I wept uncontrollably. My grief was so intense that I suffered a miscarriage. Suddenly, our child, my last remaining link to him, was gone also. Tattered and alone, I was spinning out of control, asking, "God, why me?"

At the time, I couldn't see what God was molding me into. How could He make something from such a marred mess? Not knowing what else to do with myself, I threw myself back into my work, becoming a renowned reporter, and it was in this state that I had first seen Vickie emerge from that burning building.

Now, after Vickie's ministering to me, I could look back and see that God can make a beautiful vessel glisten. Even now, He was taking me from the burned-out ruins of my life. There was more peace in my heart than I had even known. Though I would always love Guy, I also knew he was with God. God had allowed Guy to touch my life for a season. He was the key to opening my heart to accepting Jesus into my life. I realized that talking about the people God had used to touch my life would bring glory to Him.

God was using Vickie to open my eyes to my past so I could go on in peace and not in shame. She had given me a new revelation about the love of Jesus. Deceived for so long, I had hidden my past, being afraid of those who would judge me. Now I knew that God wasn't ashamed of me or what He had brought me through. How could I reach others for Jesus if I had never traveled the roads of affliction, or understood grief, pain, and sorrow?

I had now become a yielded vessel. The road to a life of love, peace, and joy usually has another road before it and that is the road of a marred vessel. I was now transformed by the hand of God into a yielded vessel, just as Vickie had stated. My past was a testimony, a story to testify about God's goodness and how He delights in molding marred vessels and healing their broken hearts.

God's power was there to guide me through the rough waters of life and was now alive within me and I was giving Him the glory. I thought back to the passage Vickie had read to me: "The fields are white unto harvest." It dawned on me that Vickie's sharing her past trials had changed my heart and perspective, so now I would be able to do the same. I could help bring in the harvest, using my past as an example for others to see Jesus high and lifted up.

Chapter Fifteen

TESTIMONIES THAT TESTIFY

After we wept in joy over my release, Vickie opened her Bible to John 4:39-41 and read: "Many of the Samaritans from the town believed in [Jesus] him because of the woman's testimony." She explained, "The testimony of the Samaritan woman at the well, who had five husbands and was living with another man, changed the lives of many in her own town. She testified about what Jesus told her; she shared the fact that He told her everything about her past and present. Jesus came to the well and this woman received the living waters of life. Her testimony brought many to Christ.

"For two days, Jesus stayed with the Samaritans. 'And because of his words many more became believers.' The love of Christ was piercing their hearts with the words He spoke to them. His prophetic message let them know that He was the Savior of the world.

"Luke 7:36-50 illustrates a testimony of love that testifies about Christ Jesus. A sinful prostitute woman anointed Jesus with costly perfume. She must have heard Jesus speak and was determined to lead a new life, for it was evident that she came out of love, and as she stood weeping, she began to wet His feet with her tears. Then, wiping His feet with her long hair, she kissed them and poured the costly perfume upon them. She still stands as a testimony that testifies about the love of Christ and her love for Him.

"Peter's is another testimony that testifies. He disowned Jesus three times before the rooster crowed. Peter stated to Jesus, in Matthew 26, 'Even if all fall away on account of you, I never will.' Jesus told him plainly that they all would leave Him and that he would verbally disown Him before the night was over. Three times Peter disowned Jesus of Nazareth. Then the rooster crowed and Peter recalled the words Jesus had spoken as he went outside and wept bitterly.

"Luke 22:31 gives us insight into the fact that Satan asked to sift Peter as wheat. Satan wanted to bring Peter to spiritual ruin here, but Jesus prayed for Peter that his faith might not fail. Peter would turn back to Jesus and strengthen other brothers in Christ. This is revealed in John 21:15-17, as Jesus reinstated Peter. Jesus asked Peter, 'Do you truly love me more than these?' 'Yes, Lord, you know that I love you,' he replied. Jesus asked again, 'Do you truly love me?' Simon Peter replied, 'Yes, Lord, you know that I love you.' The third time, Jesus said to Peter, 'Do you love me?' Peter changed his reply back to Jesus: 'Lord, You know all things; you know that I love you.'

"Peter was saying, 'I love you more than things, mankind, or myself.' He was letting Jesus know he loved Him entirely each time he replied. But then Peter answered with wisdom when he declared, 'Lord, you know all things.' This was Peter saying, 'Jesus, You see my heart; You know I love You more than self, the world, or anything it has to offer.' This was a testimony that came to testify of the faith that Peter had and of his love and devotion for Jesus that would stand and bring others to Christ.

"Satan comes to accuse the Christian brothers, to hold them in bondage, but by the blood of the Lamb and by the word of their testimony they don't love their own lives so much as to shrink from being crucified with Christ and sharing His love. We read this in Revelation 12:11.

"The word of their testimony proves their change. Their testimony testifies about Jesus to all of mankind. Their trials become a call to testify about the change God has brought about within them, thus bringing others to Him.

"Saul, also known as Paul, was forgiven and counted himself as the greatest sinner who was ever forgiven and loved by Jesus. Saul's journey in life starts at the event of Stephen being stoned to death. Saul was giving approval to Stephen being stoned to death; however, the words that Stephen cried out as he was being stoned were seeds sown. 'Lord, do not hold this against them,' declared Stephen. Truly this had to be a word that pierced the hearts of some standing there that day. Stephen spoke in love, in forgiveness, and full of the Spirit of God. Acts chapters 7-9 give us an account of the story. Saul was a murderer who had a conversion on his way to Damascus. His testimony was to testify about God and His love for all mankind."

It was a long speech, but every word of it had been filled with passion. Now Vickie's energy was spent. I sat admiring that passion and zeal. The storms of life had come, the fire had raged, but in the midst of the storms and the fires all around her, Vickie had felt the Lord's hand upon her. Her life showed me that the storms and the fires of life were all for one purpose: to refine us, to make us more like Him.

Chapter Sixteen

REFINED LIKE SILVER

The last two weeks had passed quickly. In two days, I would be back to work, and I felt like I had been refined, though I was at peace. Prior to my encounter with Vickie, I had spent my life building my own prison, keeping to myself, never allowing anyone to be a part of my life. I was now liberated from my past and the walls of my prison cell were coming down. Released from the distress of my past, I was ready to go forward in life.

Through my pain of loss, I had locked people out of my life in fear of losing them. The fear of allowing myself to love and maybe lose once again was now gone. My soul had given up its own thoughts of what to do, and had yielded itself heartily, patiently, and humbly to the working of the Spirit of God and His Word. God did a blessed work of remolding my marred past and selfish nature that had once hindered His Spirit from flowing through me.

Vickie sensed that I was at a new level of faith, and perhaps she even recognized the potential of my testimony in helping others because she began to exhort and encourage me as though she was standing before a congregation instead of simply sitting at her kitchen table talking to me.

"Listen, Anne," she said, "ask yourself if you are leaving your mark for eternity on those who cross your path in life. Abiding in unbroken fellowship with Christ, abiding in Him brings forth much fruit, fruit that will abide and touch lives.

"Picture this: God is the Potter; you're the clay vessel. God comes into the room to mold you, but you say, 'No, God, I don't like the way You're molding me; let me show You how to form me.' This inability to submit can cause a vessel to be put into the fire to remove the impurities and be refined. That refinement comes so the vessel will submit to the Maker's hand. He desires to fashion it into a yielded vessel for His purposes.

"As we allow the Spirit of God to remold us and test us, God fills us with His love and power. God empowers us yielded vessels, here in this present world, so Satan may be dethroned by the testimony of believers changing the lives of the lost and dying.

"I think back to how many times I told God, 'No, I won't do that.' It was no wonder my past was marred and my future had looked dim. But now, I've entered into submission, allowing His love to heal my past and giving Him glory for the tests and trials. I was brought into the abundance of resting in Him.

"We die to self, yet we live for Him to shine through us in all His glory. Dying to your selfish ways leads you to a life of perfect love found in the Father. Once you experience yielding yourself to the Maker's hand, you'll rest knowing He molds your earthen vessel so beautifully and completely. The place of rest is the place of abundance that is found in Him.

"The children of Israel were brought out of Egypt, to be tested for forty years — forty years in the desert, forty years of being tested before they came to the place of abundance. They were tested and refined in the heat of the desert until all the impurities had been removed from their lives, all to the glory of God. They didn't enter the Promised Land, the land of abundance, before being refined in the desert of life. This stands as a testimony that testifies about God and yielding to the Maker's hand. Their testimony gives hope and testifies to us that God loves us enough to bring us into that place of abundance in Him. God loves us so much that He allows the testing times to bring about a change of character within us so we may reflect more of Him.

"Psalm 66:10-12 states: 'For you, O God, tested us; you refined us like silver. You brought us into prison and laid burdens on our backs. You let men ride over our heads; we went through fire and water, but you brought us to a place of abundance.'

"God is not a mere passive observer of our lives, but He has His own holy purposes in allowing us to be refined like silver. The fire and the water are refining us and will stand as a testimony that will testify as we're brought into the place of His abundance.

"Burdens can be laid upon you, men may ride over you, and you may feel trapped. Though here are the words of God, He tests us to see what is in our heart. The heart needs to be refined in the fires of affliction. The storms of life and the raging seas are all there to refine you to reflect what is truly within your heart. Fire and water are metaphors for severe trials to bring about a refining of the heart so that the heart may change, becoming pure like silver."

Chapter Seventeen

REFLECTIONS

I gloried in realizing the deep joy and pleasure found in submission to God. I knew I would reflect more of Him by expressing the lessons I had learned while in the fires of affliction. The compassion that now occupied my heart was a Christlike seed planted in me that would reproduce in the lives of others. For the first time, I really understood the purpose of the lessons I had learned through hardship. My brokenness existed in order to reflect more of Him in my life and character. I could see how being refined in the fire is beautiful once you pass through and enter into that place of rest.

The song "Refiner's Fire" held a new meaning for me now. Requesting God to purify my heart is asking for God to refine that which is in me that isn't yet pure like silver or gold. When we request God to cleanse us, to make us holy, we ask for the refiner's fire or the launderer's soap. Vickie had shared with me the scripture in Malachi 3:2-3: "For he will be like a refiner's fire or a launderer's soap. He will sit as a refiner and purifier of silver; he will purify...and refine them like gold and silver. Then the LORD will have men who will bring offerings in righteousness."

Reflecting Him, reflecting His heart, reflecting His love to others, reflecting the character of Christ to those around us is the purpose of our temporary suffering. In order for me to reflect Him, I had to walk through the fires of affliction to be refined, so I could reflect His love and character to others. It was the same for Vickie. In the fire, Vickie had learned how to yield herself to Him, how to depend upon Him, how to allow the Maker to mold her as He saw fit, how to die to self and how to abide in Him.

I was so excited about the revelations that I couldn't stop bubbling over. Vickie laughed, taking great delight in my breakthrough. When I had finally talked myself out, she took up the reins of the conversation once again.

Opening her Bible to Proverbs 27:19, she read: "As water reflects a face, so a man's heart reflects the man." She explained, "The condition of one's heart indicates the individual's true character. Let your life and conduct be one of sacrificial love...love one another. As John 15:13 says: 'Greater love has no one than this, that he lay down his life for his friends.'"

"I can see that verse in you," I told her. I was thinking of that fateful day that I had seen her emerging from the fires of death into the light of day. The peace that was upon her was a mere reflection of the work that the Maker had accomplished within her heart and life. The image of her stepping out from the rubble and the ruins around her was still imprinted upon my mind. She had been willing to lay her own life aside for the sake of a small boy. God had used her to save that child, but at the same time, He had orchestrated that fire to bring the two of us together, to bring me to the place of peace and rest only found in Him. The days we had spent on this interview in her kitchen were also days of sacrifice laid down in love. Life had written her a major role, a role of bringing hope to the hurting, His love, and a testimony that spoke of her trust in God.

Vickie's lesson continued as my thoughts returned

to the sound of her voice. She was saying, "As human beings, Anne, we are so important to God that He has a blueprint in Heaven for each individual's life. Surrendered vessels are yielded to His blueprint as He charters them through their course in life. God is never careless in His creating, for He always has a plan.

"Marred vessels and yielded vessels are written about all through the Word of God. They reflect the hand of God charting their course through life, through the storms, through the fires of affliction, through it all till at last they declare, 'Nevertheless, not my will, but Yours Lord, be done.'

"In the perfect will of God, though the fire may be burning, there is a peace of mind, a peace of soul that passes all understanding. In spite of trials and hardships, you have His joy. You can rejoice in the time of battle, because you know God is the Maker, and that He is in control.

"We were made for God, in His image and likeness, and our hearts are restless until they rest in Him. Our lives are without meaning until we surrender to the Spirit of God in total submission. Hear the words, 'Not my will but Yours, Lord, be done; make me a testimony that brings glory to Your name.'

"Kathryn Kuhlman stated that Christian character isn't made on the mountaintop; it's made in the valley. She also knew the secret was yieldedness to the Lord. Reflecting His character is what life is all about.

"'We also rejoice in our sufferings, because we know that suffering produces perseverance; perseverance, character; and character, hope. And hope does not disappoint us, because God has poured out his love into our hearts by the Holy Spirit, whom he has given us' (Romans 5:3-5)."

Chapter Eighteen

GOLDEN GRAIN

Before we finally ended our interview, Vickie leaned across the table, intently looking me in the eyes, and made sure she got one point across.

"Anne, being a yielded vessel does not excuse you from trials and tribulations. Your life doesn't become automatically trouble free.

"Reaching deeper into that place of consecration and yieldedness only makes you more fit for tribulation and persecution. Trouble has a way of sneaking up on you when you least expect it. It may come without us being the direct cause of it or it may come because we're human and we fail, through either pride or error. Troubles, tribulation, and persecution have a place in shaping our lives and forming our characters.

"But we must remember, 'For our light and momentary troubles are achieving for us an eternal glory that far outweighs them all' (2 Corinthians 4:17). Tribulation works patience, for the golden grain of patience, along with the qualities of kindness, long-suffering, and love come by way of tribulation or threshing.

"The ancient thresher threshed golden wheat in order that the golden grain would separate from the sticks, stubble, and chaff. Likewise, God is after the golden grain. Threshing becomes necessary to bring forth more of Christ within the individual. We read in Luke 22:31-32 that Peter is sifted like wheat. Jesus prays that Peter's faith may not fail. When we are sifted, we should turn back and strengthen our brothers and sisters. A yielded Christian, through the indwelling of the Holy Spirit, permits troubles to become a threshing so that they may bear more of His fruit to others. The Christian's rest is found in abiding in Him in all things.

"Giving up one's entire life to Him, letting Him rule and reign, being led and taught by Him, abiding in Him, doing only what He wills for you, this is the place of rest found only in Christ Jesus."

Vickie felt compelled to share the following story with me.

"One day a young preacher was walking with an older, more seasoned preacher in a beautiful garden. The younger preacher was feeling insecure about what God had for him to do, so he was inquiring of the older preacher.

"The older preacher walked over to a beautiful rosebush and plucked a rosebud and handed it over to the young preacher, instructing him to open the rosebud without tearing off any of the delicate rose petals. With a look of disbelief the young preacher was wondering, 'What could this rosebud possibly have to do with wanting to know the will of God for my life and ministry?' However, due to the high respect the younger preacher had for the older preacher, he proceeded to unfold the delicate rosebud, attempting to keep every petal intact. In a short time he realized this was impossible to do.

"Noticing the inability of the young preacher to unfold the delicate rosebud while keeping it all intact, the older, seasoned preacher recited this poem:

It is only a tiny rosebud,
A flower by God's design;
But I cannot unfold the petals

With these clumsy hands of mine.
The secret of unfolding flowers
Is not known to such as I.
God opens the flowers so sweetly,
When in my hands they fade and die.
If I cannot unfold a rosebud,
This flower of God's design,
Then how can I think I have wisdom
To unfold this life of mine?
So I'll trust in Him for His leading
Each moment of every day.
I will look to Him for His guidance
Each step of the pilgrim way.
The pathway that lies before me
Only the heavenly Father knows.
I'll trust Him to unfold the moments,
Just as He unfolds the rose."

She paused for effect. Her words and her gaze pierced right through me.

Chapter Nineteen

HIS ROSE

We sighed almost simultaneously, both of us realizing that our time together was now coming to an end. She had planted so much into my heart and into my life. It seemed as though we had stepped outside of time for a season, and now I was finding it difficult to accept that real life was about to begin once again.

Vickie smiled at me, speaking gently in conclusion, squeezing my hand in reassurance. "His love comes into an individual and makes it blossom as a rose. He breaks up the hard ground, removing the rocks and ragged places that are hidden beneath the surface. It's His hand that transforms and unfolds the tiny rosebud into a full-blossomed rose. It is no longer I, but rather Christ living within me, unfolding my life for His glory.

"And now He's unfolding your life as well, Anne. Don't draw back from Him as He unfolds you, and you'll find yourself becoming love-ruled, love-owned, and love-motivated. It's not an easy process. The love between you and Jesus will be created and unfolded in the hard places, in the darkest hours, when you're all alone and the only one you have to call on is Him, Jesus, the lover of your soul. His love for you can produce a rose even when the tiny rosebud appears to be shut up tightly, with no sign of unfolding. He touches the rosebud of your heart in a way that only the Master's hand can. His love redeems and transforms life into beauty and usefulness."

My heart was touched. I could see that I had closed off my heart of compassion, protecting it from those around me. But now, God had removed the stony places within my heart. The selfishness that once had made me hard was gone. His Spirit had set this captive free. I had made my choice and it was clear—I was ready to love with more than mere words; I was ready to love in reality, bearing the burdens of others in love and compassion. Today I was walking in His love, because of His abounding love flowing within me.

Vickie closed her eyes and began to pray: "O Master and Maker of these earthen vessels, unfold us until we become a mirror reflection of Your love to others. No place is too hard, no sacrifice is too great, when they drive us to becoming more like You as we touch the lives of hurting people.

"When we see the abundance that You have for us, Father, in a relationship with You, we gladly submit to You and trust You to unfold each moment in our lives. You give us what our hearts have truly craved: Your perfect love. Thank You, Father. We love You. In Jesus' precious name we pray. Amen."

Warm hugs and plenty of tears accented our final parting that day. I think we both sensed that Vickie's role in my life was now over. God had used her to restore me to Himself, and now her job was done. She turned me over to Him with a glad heart.

As I drove home again, my mind returned to all the rich wisdom she had imparted to me. Tomorrow I would return to my life as a news reporter, but I was not the same person. I was a new creature in Christ. I might be going back to my previous life, but I was not going back to my former way of living. I had found the answers to the questions that had compelled me to pursue Vickie's story. If there was a personal cost to that, then it was worth paying.

I was now a beautiful rose, yielded to Him, united and utterly one with Him. I was clothed from on high with God's love. Selfishness and pride were now eliminated from within me. His love had gained ascendancy over me. My own will no longer mattered — I wanted His will.

All of the teachings of my youth suddenly made sense in light of all I had learned from Vickie's story. Jesus, our perfect example, had come in the form of man to teach us all how to submit to God, our Maker. Jesus had loved Judas even knowing that Judas had already stolen from Him and was plotting to sell Him for thirty pieces of silver. Jesus had loved the man who drove the nails into His hands and feet. Jesus had loved the Roman soldiers who flogged Him and mocked and ridiculed Him. He had let love rule Him in all things. That same love puts a fragrance within our lives; the sweet smell of a rose in full blossom comes only from the Master's hand.

As yielded vessels, which were marred vessels, we learn to rest in the hands of the Maker as He unfolds our lives. The God of rest, peace, and love rests within our entire beings. Jesus the lover is unveiled within us. God's love sets us in a place where we can shine His light into the lives of the ungodly and the brothers in Christ who are hurting. The miracle of His love transforms the rosebud into a rose as He unfolds our lives in His hands.

God alone knows the secret of unfolding flowers, and He unfolds them so beautifully. Vickie had related to me how she had tried to unfold her own life at times, thus tearing the delicate petals in the process. Now she used the story of her life as a testimony that testifies about God, giving Him glory for unfolding her as she learned to trust Him in all things. She truly was His rose in the garden of life sent from God to touch my life with His love.

I would never be the same, for my eyes were opened, and my heart was changed. It was the story I needed to hear for my own life, and God had used her to heal me. Now He would begin to use me to heal others.

To contact the author:
Life Touch Ministries
P.O. Box 306
Claremore, OK 74018-0306
(918)379-0220

www.lifetouchministries.org